TRUSTING GOD TO GET YOU
THROUGH

JASON CRABB

Charisma
HOUSE
A STRANG COMPANY

MOST STRANG COMMUNICATIONS BOOK GROUP products are available at special quantity discounts for bulk purchase for sales promotions, premiums, fund-raising, and educational needs. For details, write Strang Communications Book Group, 600 Rinehart Road, Lake Mary, Florida 32746, or telephone (407) 333-0600.

TRUSTING GOD TO GET YOU THROUGH by Jason Crabb
Published by Charisma House, A Strang Company
600 Rinehart Road, Lake Mary, Florida 32746
www.strangbookgroup.com

Cover design by Justin Evans
Design Director: Bill Johnson

Visit the author's website at www.jasoncrabb.com.

Library of Congress Cataloging-in-Publication Data
Crabb, Jason.
  Trusting God to get you through / Jason Crabb. -- 1st ed.
      p. cm.
  ISBN 978-1-61638-174-5
  1. Christian life. 2. Trust in God--Christianity. 3. Crabb, Jason.
I. Title.
  BV4637.C69 2010
  248.4--dc22
                                    2010038998

E-book ISBN: 978-1-61638-397-8

First Edition

11 12 13 14 15 — 9 8 7 6 5 4 3 2 1
Printed in the United States of America

Jason Crabb has been through the fire and has come out with a very wonderful thing—a testimony of God's faithfulness! You will be inspired to a new level of faith as you read *Trusting God to Get You Through*.

—Jim Cymbala
Pastor, The Brooklyn Tabernacle

It was my blessing and pleasure to read Jason's book. It's powerful reading, because he shares personal experiences and thoughts and then quotes God's Word. I'm not only a fan of Jason's extraordinary singing and his captivating television personality, but I'm also a fan of him as an author.

I love that he comes from a musical family, too!

—Barbara Mandrell
Award-winning country music singer

Getting to know Jason Crabb over the past couple of years has been an uplifting and inspiring experience. He is truly a Spirit-filled man and one of the greatest singers and musicians in any musical genre. You can hear and feel the anointing of God when he sings. On or off stage, Jason encourages, prays for, or offers a helping hand to everyone he meets. Like King David, Jason Crabb is a man after God's own heart.

—William Lee Golden
Singer, the Oak Ridge Boys

When believers sit under the ministry of both speakers and singer, they often have a misconception that their lives are sort of a "Cinderella and the Prince" story. They imagine a life free from cares, restrained from attacks and demonic activity, and living a paradise on Earth. Many are unaware that the songs and messages are birthed from the times of travail, trials, and testing they have endured and overcome.

In Jason's book *Trusting God to Get You Through* you will not only read the inside, personal stories that have helped mold the man of God and undergird his faith in difficult times, but Jason will give clear nuggets and personal insight that will help you to get through your own seasons of difficulty. You will be blessed and encouraged!

—Perry Stone
Best-selling author of *Secrets From Beyond the Grave*

A great book about a young man God has blessed with one of the best voices I have ever heard, and he uses it to promote his Christian beliefs.

—Bill Carter
Executive producer of *The Gaither Gospel Hour* and more than one dozen *Gaither Homecoming Specials*, and former manager for Reba McEntire and Lonestar

I don't have to say much about Jason's voice. Anyone who's ever heard it can feel his conviction as he sings. In his new book, *Trusting God to Get You Through*, he shares with the reader just how deep that conviction really goes. [He offers] powerful stories of the joys and sorrows of everyday life but with the promise of God that He will help you through. Bravo Jason! A very encouraging word!

—KEN HARDING
PRESIDENT, NEW HAVEN RECORDS

"Well, we all knew Jason Crabb could sing. But if you haven't heard the news, get this: he can write, too! The lessons Jason has learned (some, the hard way) are told in the stories of his life as a son, a husband, a father—a boy and a man. Jason's heart fills the pages of this book with hope for the hopeless and love for the lost. Put aside what you have been reading and turn your attention to this book right now. It is just that powerful.

—ANDY ANDREWS
NEW YORK TIMES BEST-SELLING AUTHOR OF THE NOTICER

Trusting God to Get You Through is a wonderful collection of Jason's life-long experiences, highlighted with God's holy Word, to describe how he and his family have made it through life thus far. It is an inspirational, motivational, and encouraging message written for us to understand how we too can make it through. Jason is truly a man of God serving Him through song, service, and word. My wife, Pam, and I were moved by his honesty to share his life with others so that we too can make it through this worldly life.

Jason uses his talents, but he always hides behind the cross of Christ in doing it. God bless you and yours, Jason!

—DAVID HALE
COFOUNDER OF KNIGHT AND HALE GAME CALLS

Jason Crabb has done a remarkable job of sharing his and the Crabb Family's faith and personal history with us. In *Trusting God to Get You Through*, Jason's passion for ministry is evident. His book is not just a simple autobiography; it is a personal testimony that gives God all the glory and brings hope and encouragement to the reader. This book ministered to me in a powerful way. Thank you, Jason!

—VICTORIA HEARST
PRESIDENT/FOUNDER PRAISE HIM MINISTRIES

Jason Crabb is a born communicator. Whether he's belting out a powerful song with that amazing voice, sharing a conversation with a fan after a concert, or writing this wonderful book, Jason has a gift for encouraging and inspiring those around him. Jason Crabb is a young man with a lot to say, and we're all blessed when he shares his heart.

—DEBORAH EVANS PRICE
AUTHOR OF THE COUNTRY MUSIC ASSOCIATION AWARDS VAULT
AND FREELANCE JOURNALIST FOR BILLBOARD, COUNTRY WEEKLY,
AOL'S THE BOOT, AND OTHER OUTLETS

To my family, for the experiences
we have shared and the countless
ways that you have helped to shape
my life, I am forever grateful
and dedicate this book to you.

ACKNOWLEDGMENTS

SO MANY SPECIAL people have contributed to the experiences involved in writing this book. Thanks to Shellye, my lifelong companion and forever reminder of God's amazing ways; Ashleigh and Emma, God's gift of perfect love; Philip and Tina, my right hand and the very picture of God's faithfulness; my road crew, David and Lorie Sikes, Michael Rowsey, and Stephanie Reece (with a hearty welcome to Blaine Johnson, the newest member of our traveling "family"); Jerrel Parten, my faithful, confident, steadfast supporter during pivotal times for this ministry; Kellye Addison, master of the details who keeps the wheels turning daily; Donna Scuderi, who labored tirelessly to enhance this book with her insights and creativity; and Barbara Dycus, Ann Mulchan, and the entire Strang Communications team for your excellent support.

THROUGH THE FIRE

So many times I've questioned certain circumstances
Things I could not understand
Many times in trials, weakness blurs my vision
Then my frustration gets so out of hand
It's then I am reminded I've never been forsaken
I've never had to stand the test alone
As I look at all the victories the spirit rises up in me
And it's through the fire my weakness is made strong!
He never promised that the cross would not get heavy
And the hill would not be hard to climb!
He never offered our victories without fighting
But He said help would always come in time!
Just remember when you're standing in the valley of
    decision
And the adversary says, "Give in!"
Just hold on, our Lord will show up
And He will take you through the fire again!
I know within myself that I would surely perish
But if I trust the hand of God, He'll shield the flames
    again.

—GERALD CRABB, "THROUGH THE FIRE"

CONTENTS

FOREWORD

I DISTINCTLY REMEMBER THE first time I ever heard Jason Crabb sing. It was before our concert in Memphis. Jason and his siblings were there, and someone told me, "You've got to hear these kids sing!" After hearing their wonderful sound, I put them on the program that night, and over the next few years I included them more and more.

After the Crabb Family stopped traveling as a group, Jason was singing solo, and I invited him to sing with the Gaither Vocal Band and the Homecoming Tour numerous times. The more I got to know him, the more I could see that everything this kid *appears* to be when you first meet him is genuinely who he is: guileless, talented, infectious, energetic, and passionate about reflecting Christ's Spirit through his life and his music. I have never met a kid quite like him.

If character flaws are going to surface, they will most likely surface after long, grueling days in the studio or during hours and hours spent in the confined space of a bus during a long ride. Yet in those situations, Jason's attitude and humility have only proven his authenticity.

I get a bit nervous when I see a kid so young who possesses this much ability and charisma, because it takes a great amount of inward character to withstand the attention that comes with that much talent. But Jason's character remains unshaken. He is truly a joy to be around.

This young man has been through some very deep waters, and he will talk about some of those experiences in this book. To see how He has allowed God to use those circumstances to refine him, even at his young age, is a testament to this dear artist's heart for Christ. The way he honors his Savior, as well as his wife and children, after all he has been through is very refreshing.

When the gospel music industry lost Glen Payne, we lost a great spirit and a cheerleader for other artists. He truly rejoiced when other artists succeeded. But Jason Crabb's giant spirit and genuine happiness for others' success is carrying on that part of Glen's legacy, perhaps as no other artist I know.

God is using this young man, and I have a feeling this is only the beginning for Jason Crabb.

—BILL GAITHER
SINGER, SONGWRITER, AUTHOR,
MUSICIAN, COMPOSER, DIRECTOR

PREFACE

MORE THAN ANYTHING else, this book is about an amazing God who reaches down and touches ordinary lives. It is a testimony of all He has done for my family and for the people we have been privileged to meet throughout our years on the road. I pray it is an encouragement to you and to anyone who wonders, as I have, why certain things happen the way they do.

I wrote this book because every soul walks *through the fire* of adversity. Most of us have walked that plank several times. Whether the life of your dreams is unfolding before your eyes or you are losing hope that it ever will, you have tasted a trial or two. No human being with breath in his lungs can say, "Difficulty has never darkened my doorstep."

The Crabb family is just like your family. We have known a lot of love and our fair share of struggles. Our parents jumped through the same hoops as all people who get married or start a family or have a calling. My siblings and I experienced the same challenges faced by children of all ages all over the world—we have a funny last name (and it cost us!), we started out with nothing and lived without, and we experienced divorce.

My mom and dad are wonderful people. I couldn't ask for better parents and mentors than they are to me and my siblings. They are strong, honest people who have worked hard and helped others. They love God, they love us kids, and they love serving the kingdom. Like many couples, they did their best, and still, their marriage came apart. Like all couples, they made mistakes and learned from them. And, like the rest of us, they are imperfect people—the reason Jesus was born in a manger.

Divorce is *hard*—hard for couples, hard for children. *Hard*. No one wants to experience it or see their kids go through it. I won't kid you; the divorce of my parents made for difficult transitions, individually and as a family. My mom and dad shouldered a lot before, during, and after their divorce. We all did. It looked like the perfect setup for destruction. If not for God and my parents' tenacity and devotion to us kids, I don't know how it would have ended.

Which brings me back to the reason I wrote this book: You and I may have entirely different life experiences. Yet, when we look in the rearview mirror, we can see the high points and low points of days gone by. The important thing—the truly *amazing* thing— is that we came through all of it. There may be a scar or two to remind us of the past, but the past is behind us.

More than that is this fact: we came through it *for a reason*. There is something God is yet going to do with us. You may not be called to gospel singing, but God has something in mind for you. Whatever you have gone through or are facing today, I know this: "In all things God works for the good of those who love him, who have been called according to his purpose" (Rom. 8:28).

I know this because He has proven it over and over again in my life. He turned painful circumstances into more of His goodness. Instead of having two loving parents and three siblings, I ended up with my mom, dad, stepmom, and stepdad—and more siblings with whom I could grow and bond. I know all of them love me very much, and I know I love them with all my heart. I may not have chosen the trials my family endured, but I wouldn't rewrite the course of my life or trade my family for anything!

God did all of this *and* gave us a ministry to fulfill in His name! He didn't do it because we can sing or because we toughed out the hard times; He did it because He is a loving God who causes all things to work together for our good, no matter the circumstances...no matter our fears.

God is "no respecter of persons" (Acts 10:34, KJV). You may be called to the halls of finance, the classroom, or the pulpit; you may be an artisan, a homemaker, or an office worker. Whatever your experiences—joys or sorrows—our amazing God can use every bit of your life to produce the most unexpected results.

That is my story. It is your story too.

GOING WITH GOD

IT'S SOMETHING I'VE always known. I never had to wonder or figure it out. There's never been a question in my mind; I was born to sing. It's what I was created to do and part of what makes me tick. Singing is embedded in my nature. I have sung ever since I could walk, or even stand.

THE SINGING CRABB FAMILY

Singing runs in my family. Looking back, I'm amazed at the experiences we have had because of it. Yet it all started in simple ways and from humble beginnings. It started with my parents. Mom and Dad have great voices, and both of them sang at church. They shared a love for music; over the years, our whole family was drawn to singing.

Our beginnings were rough-and-tumble. So was my Dad's childhood. As far as anyone could tell, he was growing up with the deck stacked against him. Financial woes made for a chaotic youth and unstable housing arrangements. Not only was his family poor, but also Dad's father was an alcoholic. At some point, the wear and tear took their toll, and Dad's parents divorced. Things only got worse for Dad and his sisters.

At eighteen, Mom and Dad got married. By the time I was about fourteen they separated. Before long, Dad was a divorcee who had turned to alcohol. The situation was tough on Mom too, but God had better things in store. Both my parents found love again. Mom married Timmy, who is a great guy, and Dad married a terrific woman named Kathy.

Despite their trials, my parents grew spiritually stronger day by day, and Dad got delivered from alcohol! Our family grew too—literally overnight. Like any blended family, we faced challenges, yet we became knitted together to the point that bloodlines disappeared. We were simply brothers and sisters who loved each other. As harmonious as our family was (no pun intended!), a larger family didn't make things any easier, especially for my parents.

Dad's lack of formal education made it hard to find good work, yet his musical gifts outmatched any deficits in schooling. Music had always been a mainstay in our family. Throughout my childhood, the whole family sang at home. I can remember being four or five years old and living in a trailer in Beaver Dam, Kentucky. There wasn't a whole lot to do. We weren't able to travel, and we didn't have fancy toys or big-screen TVs. What we had was music. It was good, clean fun, and it didn't cost anything. Whatever was going on around us, music was something we could enjoy as a family.

Music wasn't the only passion of the Crabb kids. My brothers and I were huge fans of the Wildcats, the University of Kentucky's basketball team. If you had asked us about our dreams during those years, we would have told you that we dreamed of being on the hardwood with the Wildcats.

We didn't have cable or satellite TV in those days, so whenever our team was on TV, we would wrap the rabbit ears of our indoor antenna with aluminum foil and hope to get reception. Sometimes it worked, and sometimes it didn't. But on any given day, whether in the blistering heat or the winter cold, you could find the Crabb boys on the cow pasture, dribbling the ball away from the cows' "business" and shooting three-pointers into a basket we had jerry-rigged on a pole.

Our love of basketball was so strong, yet the musical thread continued to weave its way through our lives. We didn't know at the time that God was grooming us for the unimaginable things He had planned. We had certainly never imagined the day we would be asked to sing the national anthem on the basketball court at the University of Kentucky!

In those early days when we thought we were just having fun singing songs, we were really in boot camp, learning to sing and harmonize and perform for others. I recall a particular time when I was just a boy; I began thinking up lyrics, so I shared them with my dad. The words were simple, but I still remember them:

Jesus, we love You,
We love You so much.
You came to take us to heaven,
Jesus, Jesus, how we love You so much.

As I sang my song, Dad encouraged me to keep going. In fact, he recorded me singing the song. I have the tape to this day. I can also remember times later on when Dad and I would stay up nights recording the songs he wrote. We would lay down tracks one instrument at a time on whatever equipment we had.

Eventually, Dad began writing songs on a regular basis, and we all got involved singing them. It wasn't something we planned. It was more like a key had turned in the heavens, and we walked through the door. Unexpected opportunities to sing in public began opening up to us. We sang in a small community church, but our ministry soon grew beyond the church walls. New venues began to invite us, and before long, ministry took us to places far from home.

Our family ministry continued to grow stronger as we traveled together. It wasn't a glamorous life, but it *was* glorious. We were astounded by the things God did in our midst. I remember one of the first times we sang a song called "Please Forgive Me," and thirty-eight people gave their hearts to Christ! It was overwhelming to see God move in such a powerful way through the simple words of a song.

The not-so-glorious side of ministry life is also memorable; the moments of irony help to keep us balanced through the highs and lows of living and traveling in the public eye. A perfect example is the day someone called to tell us that our song "Please Forgive Me" was number one on the charts. At the exact moment we received the good news, our bus was stuck in a parking lot with a flat tire!

Another *balancing* experience involved a wonderful but grueling Christmas road tour. We really did it up with special lights and props to evoke the season. With all the extra gear loaded into a truck, we drove from concert to concert, setting up the lights and sound system, doing the concert, and then tearing down the whole stage setup into the wee hours. We did everything ourselves and repeated the process night after night with little sleep and not a moment to catch our breath. The ministry was outstanding, but I won't lie: we were so worn out, we thought about making a bonfire of all that extra gear when the tour was over!

MINISTRY 101

Getting a ministry off the ground isn't easy. We had to become jacks of all trades, doing whatever was needed to answer the call and fulfill approximately three hundred concerts per year. To maintain such a rigorous schedule, we did without life's amenities. We bathed at truck stops—in showers if they had them, in sinks when they didn't. We hoped for hotel rooms but did without them most of the time. We hauled and set up our own equipment and then broke it down—every single show.

For years, we arranged our travel schedule to include a regular monthly concert in Owensboro, Kentucky, which was pretty near to our hometown. We did all our own publicity and maintained a mailing list of five or six thousand names. For each mailing, we had to lick thousands of postage stamps and hang posters in Beaver Dam and anyplace else we could think of. Having to do everything ourselves kept us busy all the time. When we weren't singing, we were stuffing letters. When we weren't driving, we were changing the oil. When the tune-up was finished, there were telephone calls to make. It was a ton of work—and still is. But all of it has been worth it, because the bottom line has always been about people hearing the message of the gospel.

Considering our beginnings, our developing story is an unexpected one. For sure, we could not have concocted it on our own. It has been a God thing all the way. It is not a story about a particular family but about how He can take even desperate circumstances and use them for His glory.

For reasons of His own, God has used our lives as living testimonies of His goodness. He's still doing it, in new ways and through different circumstances. Yet with every step He has given us something to encourage us—some kind of heavenly stamp of approval that keeps us on track. Whether by providing a new tire or a new bus, bringing mentors into our lives, or giving us favor with those He would use to expand our ministry, God has shown us at every turn that He is the One who is backing us up and moving us forward. Over the years, He has faithfully led us into situations and relationships He designed to produce lasting fruit. It is just as Jesus told His disciples, "You did not choose me, but I chose you and appointed you to go and bear fruit—fruit that will last" (John 15:16).

So many experiences come to mind; all of them attest to His love. I'll share many of them in the pages ahead. For now, the long and short of it is this: everything we have lived through has been part of a much bigger picture than we could have envisioned. Just as He does for each and every one of His children, God has a plan for the Crabb clan. The beginning of His plan preceded our lifetimes, and the end of the plan is nowhere in sight. We just keep on taking it one day at a time, determined to keep going with God.

CHANGE IS PART OF THE PLAN

The Crabb Family hit the road when I was sixteen. For the next fifteen years, traveling was the only life I knew or could imagine. I loved the way we worked together; everything seemed to fit like a glove. The love that knitted us together through years of transition laid a solid foundation for us as a ministry family. Everyone had a role, and everyone was ready to pitch in wherever help was needed.

Whenever a question arose, we kids could rely on our parents for wisdom and the right solution. They taught us so much! Whether we realized it or not, my siblings and I were learning how to flow in the Holy Spirit, what to say and when to say it, what to do and what not to do. Day by day, we soaked in our parents' instruction, learning what we needed to know so that we could do whatever had to be done.

Yet, even as we matured in our understanding and confidence, we took comfort in knowing that our parents were guiding us. They provided a strong backstop against anything that might go wrong. Even if all hell broke loose on the road or onstage, we knew they could keep us moving in the right direction as a family and as a ministry. I guess you could say that our nest was well feathered. We were comfortable and secure with our parents at the helm.

In God's plan, that kind of safe living can't last forever. The day came when our comfy nest was plucked, and, like eaglets whose time for flight has come, my siblings and I were thrust forward. Dad announced that he was coming off the road. By 2003, both he and Kathy had retired from touring. My siblings and I were faced with an alarming prospect: we would have to take the reins or leave the road behind.

It wasn't as though we hadn't been prepared for their retirement. We knew the ropes. Yet, knowing what to do was one thing; actually doing it on our own was another. Perched on the edge of the nest, high above the ground, we knew that climbing back under the feathers wasn't an option. The time had come for the Crabb kids to face their moment of truth. We had to decide whether we would retreat or take flight. Either way, our lives were going to change.

By the grace of God, we chose to keep going with God. We faced the fear of the unknown, wondering exactly how things would work out. At times, it was a game of inches, yet everything worked out just fine. We carried on the ministry and put into practice everything we had learned—and then some!

Once we recovered from the initial shock of being on our own, we found the groove and rhythm of walking it out. There was a little nervousness at first, and we encountered some obstacles. For one thing, we had to recalibrate our individual roles. As siblings in a seamlessly blended family that had no favorites, we had always operated as equals. Yet, somebody had to take the lead. I guess because I was the oldest of the siblings on the road, that somebody was me. We were still equals—all for one and one for all—but my brothers and sisters now looked for me to be more of a leader. Stepping up to a new level is always a challenge, but God reassured us. Just as He always had, He gave His sweet stamp of approval. We saw hearts transformed before our eyes, we saw new doors open to us, we developed a more youthful musical style, and we received professional recognition straight out of the gate. Our albums *The Walk, Driven,* and *Live at Brooklyn Tabernacle* were nominated for Grammy awards, and five songs from those albums won Dove awards. All of it was God's way of saying, "I'm still blessing what's going on."

The way things turned out was stunning. Considering the logistics of the transition, including the shifts in our individual roles, our venture out of the nest could have turned into a nightmare. Instead, we locked arms, moved as a unit, and by God's grace, never missed a beat. Our skills as a blended family helped us to avoid the pitfalls of competition and strife. We loved each other, supported one another, and were committed to doing ministry together until Jesus returned.

Everything about it seemed right. We continued to minister all over the United States, tallying up a total of fifteen years on the road together. All the cylinders were firing, yet change would find us once again. This change would be even more radical than the previous one.

God's Transforming Touch

Like everything in life, change is part of the growth process and the fulfillment of God's will. Whether in nature or personal development, "There is a time for everything, and a season for every activity under heaven" (Eccles. 3:1).

This has certainly proven true in our family. In 2007, a new season dawned for us, one that is unfolding even now. It had begun in our hearts individually and was ignited by God with an unexpected spark at a specific point in time—a birthday celebration for a beloved man of God.

The bash was for Pastor Rod Parsley's fiftieth birthday in January 2007. Many people joined in the celebration; the pews were packed. My brothers and sisters and I enjoyed the goings on from the platform with Clint Brown, Donnie McClurkin, and some other folks.

It was the most dynamic birthday party I had ever seen. We had ourselves some church that night!

Pastor Parsley didn't just sit back and soak up the birthday wishes. Instead, he went down front and prayed for people—specifically for everybody in the house. And I mean *everybody*. When he had finished praying for the last person, he came up on the platform and prayed for some of us singers. Soon, he made his way over to me.

What happened next was life changing. Rod Parsley called me out, looked me dead in the eye, and said, "You're going to venture out to different things. There's going to be a time change in your life." With that, he removed his watch from his wrist and put it on mine.

The weight of God's glory in that moment drove me to my knees. What Rod Parsley didn't know was that God had already been dealing with us about change. He was pointing my siblings and me toward a future that made all of us uneasy. For some time, we had been sensing that He was calling us away from a single family ministry. We'd had glimpses of a new season in which all of us would climb out of the nest yet again and fly in separate ministry directions. This vision was clear enough that we were getting ready to announce that the Crabb Family would disband in about a year's time.

Though we understood God's call to some degree, questions remained. So did the uncomfortable sense of the unknown. We wouldn't be traveling on the same bus anymore or singing together each night. The very things we had always done were about to end. We wondered how that could be *right* and how in the world it would work. We needed some kind of indisputable confirmation; we needed God's stamp of approval assuring us that these thoughts were His thoughts. Now, in the midst of a birthday celebration, that confirmation had come straight from heaven.

As I fell to my knees, I cried out to God. The decision we had made was the right one, but the implications were hard to digest. My heart was heavy—really heavy. A lot of questions and situations faced us. The coming transition would test our mettle. The prophetic word Pastor Parsley brought was filled with hope, but he knew nothing of the issues we saw coming. We didn't know the half of it ourselves. Nor did we have to. Rod Parsley's words had served their purpose; they were the warm salve of assurance that the Father was pleased. It was clear that despite the changes ahead we were still going with God.

I can barely describe the magnitude of the prophecy's effect. Not only did it calm my fears, but it also reminded me of the lengths to which God will go to show His love to His kids. For one thing, the watch placed on my wrist would serve as a symbol (as it does to this day) of God's will and purpose for my life. Add to that the manner in which God chose to speak—it left an imprint on my heart! I was overwhelmed by the fact that He chose a man with the influence and voice of Rod Parsley to speak into our lives. (I continue to be amazed at the people God sends our way!)

I thank God for the clarity of His confirmation that night, because, after fifteen years of singing, ministering, and preaching as a family, it was tough to go in separate directions. It was hard to see myself going solo; it was a concept way outside the box of my thinking. Yet God said, "It's time—time to let everybody grow into what I want them to be, time to let them experience leadership in the direction I have for them."

We needed to set aside our skepticism and *stretch*. I had to believe that a solo ministry would work. My siblings needed to know that they'd be all right without me by their sides. It was important to me that the right things happen for my brothers and sisters. I felt a certain amount of responsibility for their success through another tough transition. So, when they were signed to record deals and became excited about the future, I knew everything was going to be OK.

SONG OF ENCOURAGEMENT

Looking back, I can see how God's perfect plan, will, and purpose have unfolded since that moment. His touch on my life changed everything, and because of it, I have a passion to touch the lives of others. I sense this call now more than ever. With so much uncertainty in our world and with so many people hurting and living with their backs literally against the wall due to job losses and shrinking retirement funds, many are tempted to give up.

You might be tempted to give up too.

That's why I wrote this book. It is my song of encouragement to tell you, "Don't quit! The biggest and brightest blessings are on the other side of the struggle." You may be in the most intense firestorm of your life. The flames may be licking at your heels in every area. The heat may feel as fierce as a California wildfire raging from ridge to ridge across the foothills.

Yet, as bad as things might be, God tells us that we can make it with His help. He encourages us to keep going with Him! Hebrews 10:36 says it in words as plain as they can be: "You need to persevere so that when you have done the will of God, you will receive what he has promised."

Simple words like these from the writer of Hebrews reach me. They take hold in my heart in those moments when it seems nothing else can. It is similar to the way the right song can affect me; it has the power to reach inside and pinpoint the issue or concern lodged in my heart.

God often uses songs to speak to me. One of my favorites is a song my dad wrote. The title says it all: "Through the Fire." My family has sung it countless times. We have seen it touch lives. It has ministered to me during crisis times in my own life. Now, as you turn these pages, I suspect it will touch yours, maybe for the first time.

For me, the most rewarding part of ministry is to help someone who is going "through the fire." I cannot explain the fulfillment it brings. I can only say that, no matter how hard the work or how tough the schedule, I relish every opportunity to touch lives. It is the reason my family perseveres and keeps going. We want others to know that God will keep them. He will protect them, not always *from* the storm but *in* the storm.

My desire is for God to touch your life as you read this book. My hope is for you see your story in these pages and to summon the courage to trust Him in the midst of the fire, knowing that He will always be found at your side, even when you are surrounded by flames. He did it for three young Hebrew men centuries ago. (See Daniel 3.) He will do it for you too.

Before long, you *will* come out of the fire.

*Just hold on, our Lord
will show up*

*And He will take you
through the fire again!*

*...Trust the hand of God,
He'll shield the flames again.*

Chapter 1

Facing Life's Questions

*So many times I've questioned
certain circumstances*

Things I could not understand.

GRACE THROUGH THE FIRE

EVERY SONG I sing has lyrics centered on a strong gospel message, although the sounds are similar to musical genres that are popular today. Sometimes those familiar styles open doors to exciting and unexpected opportunities to sing outside of mainstream gospel circles.

I'm jazzed by invitations to take part in nontraditional gospel events. One such invite led to the stage of the Grand Ole Opry, a place like no other in the world. Just being on that stage is an honor; how that particular night played out—well, it added to my amazement and demonstrated God's willingness to use unusual circumstances in the fulfillment of His will.

Talk about irony! The sponsor of our portion of that night's program was a watering hole in Nashville. You heard me right; our segment was sponsored by a bar—and what an amazing night it turned out to be. From that iconic stage I was privileged to share a testimony that was fresh in my heart.

"Through the Fire" was part of my testimony that night. Like all my dad's songs, it speaks to experiences that are common to all people. The song has run like a thread through the fabric of my own life. I told the audience at the Grand Ole Opry as much, explaining how the song had ministered to Shellye and me during a painful season.

It was a poignant moment when I shared how God had brought us through the trauma of losing two precious babies in separate miscarriages. Although the shock of those losses was still fresh in our thoughts, fresher still was the miracle of God in bringing our season of heartbreak to an end. That night—February 14, 2003—I had the pleasure of sharing *breaking news* from our house: Shellye and I had just experienced the birth of our first child! Our daughter, Ashleigh Taylor, had been born the day before, and she and her momma were doing just fine.

After the audience heard our songs and our testimony about Ashleigh's birth, a woman stopped us outside the auditorium. Like most everyone else at the Opry, she had come to hear the music. But God had more than music in mind for her. With tears streaming down her face, she said, "I didn't have any idea I was coming here for this tonight, but I rededicated my life to God—right here at the Grand Ole Opry—sponsored by a bar!"

Life doesn't always follow the script that makes sense to us. That was true for this woman, and it was true of our miscarriages. The birth of Ashleigh had come after many long days of testing and trial. So many times the dream of raising a family seemed bound in thick layers of impossibility. Yet deep down, Shellye and I knew that we were not alone in the fight. God's Word told us so. Many nights the Scriptures comforted and strengthened us. We had His assurance that He would bring us through:

> When you pass through the waters,
>   I will be with you;
> and when you pass through the rivers,
>   they will not sweep over you.
> When you walk through the fire,
>   you will not be burned;
>   the flames will not set you ablaze.
> For I am the LORD, your God.
>
> —ISAIAH 43:2–3

Shellye and I walked through some fire. Yet God brought us out and blessed us—radically! Today we have two daughters, Ashleigh Taylor and Emmaleigh Love. They are as beautiful as can be, just like their mother. I will tell you more about them later, but first let me tell you about the love of my life.

MY COWGIRL

My earliest awareness of Shellye came when someone brought me a picture of her and said, "You've got to meet this girl."

My reaction was, "Yeah, she's kind of cute. Yeah, I'd like to meet her."

I guess I played down my curiosity in front of my friend, but I thought the girl in the picture was beautiful. Little did I know that someone had shown that beautiful girl a picture of me. It was a shot from the album *Looking Ahead,* a record our family made even before we started singing full-time. I had a crazy hairdo at the time—a comb-over with a curl that dropped right down the center of my forehead. My hairstyle looked like a 1950s throwback. Shellye wasn't impressed.

Her reaction was actually stronger than that. She looked at the photo and said, "No way. I don't think I'd like him at all."

She then pointed to my curl, saying, "I don't know about that."

Sometime later, the Crabb Family was invited by Kentucky Educational Television (KET) to be part of an outdoor concert in Rosine, Kentucky, the home of bluegrass and the birthplace of Bill Monroe, the man known to this day as the Father of Bluegrass Music.[1] KET asked us to sing for a documentary they were making about Kentucky music.

Friends had told me ahead of time that Shellye planned to come and see me at the concert. Things didn't go exactly according to plan, however. She and her folks arrived after our set was over. We were headed off the stage when I spotted Shellye getting out of a car.

I never took my eyes off her; I watched her walk across the field and toward the stage. I might not be able to tell you what Shellye wore yesterday, but I can tell you exactly what she was wearing in Rosine. She cut straight across that field in blue jeans, a flannel shirt, and roper boots.

Shellye was the prettiest girl I had ever seen. She looked even more beautiful than her picture. My heart skipped a beat—maybe two—and I remember thinking, "Well, I've got me a little cowgirl with long, curly hair."

I wasn't the only one who noticed Shellye. Our drummer asked, "Who is that?"

I said, "Let's go meet her."

"Yeah, I want to meet her," he said.

We talked to Shellye for a while. Then it hit me: I didn't need to help the drummer get to know Shellye; I needed to head him off at the pass! Just as quick as you can bat an eye, I asked her, "Hey, what are you doing tonight?"

"I'm going to church," she replied.

"Well, good, because I'm going with you."

I didn't ask her *if* I could accompany her; I just told her we were going to church together. It was bold, but it was OK with Shellye. She was comfortable knowing that her stepmom knew me. In fact, her stepmom was Kathy's cousin. So, I wasn't a complete stranger, and church seemed like a safe first date.

In the meantime, we tried to get out of the blistering heat. The only place that was even slightly cooler than that hot Kentucky field was the inside of our old GMC bus. It was our family's first bus, and it burned almost as much oil as it did gas. It wasn't pretty, but it had places to sit and offered shelter from the sun. It even had a recliner that we had installed for on-the-road comfort.

Shellye sat in the recliner, and I stood in the stairwell. We just talked and talked until it was night. By the time we left for church, one thing was certain: our meeting was no accident. The hours I spent with Shellye were like nothing I had ever experienced. We were clearly drawn to one another and found it easy to talk and laugh together. It sounds like a cliché, but we felt almost as though we had known each other for some time.

That night, Shellye and I went to church. At some point, I learned that she was seeing someone, but the relationship was not serious. The next day, the fellow Shellye had dated called her before I did. She refused to come to the phone. She had already decided that she didn't want to talk to anyone but me.

When I finally called, it was Shellye's turn to be bold. She asked me whether I was coming over and said she wanted to see me again. I didn't have to think twice about my answer. I just said, "I'll come over."

When I got to Shellye's house, she and her twin sister answered the door. Seeing the two of them caught me by surprise, but I got over it. There was no doubt in my mind: there was only one Shellye, and she was the girl for me.

The memories of those days are strong. The slightest reminder can trigger my senses and transport me back in time. During our courtship, I made it a habit to pick up some watermelon gum and a Dr. Pepper on my way to Shellye's house. To this day, the sight, smell, or taste of either one affects us, and each year the first October breeze reminds us of the day we met.

My Better Half

Years ago, I prayed and asked God to bring the right woman into my life. I knew it was important to find not just *a* good woman but *the* right woman. God answered my prayers. Shellye is everything I need and everything I am not. She helps me to remain rooted in what matters. She helps me to strike a healthy balance between family and ministry. She helps me to stay grounded when I'm on the road.

Shellye is an amazing wife and mother and the perfect helpmate. Of course, she is much more than that. Ask anyone about Shellye, and they will tell you that she is a rock. In fact, that's what they call her: *the rock*. She is content in life. She is comfortable with our roles and all they entail. She is supportive of me while at the same time fulfilled as a stay-at-home mom. Her deep contentment brings me peace. I know that when I'm on the road, I don't have to worry about her or my kids. Shellye has it all in hand.

Not everyone who travels enjoys the kind of homecomings I do. Not every spouse can deal with the things Shellye takes in stride. Keeping the home fires burning is not a chore for my wife. When I return from a stint on the road, I enter a home bubbling over with warmth and love. It is inviting and reassuring and demonstrates Shellye's wholeness. Her joy is a great blessing to our family. As a man,

I can't imagine a better home life than the one I've got. As a father, I can't imagine a better mother for Ashleigh and Emmaleigh.

One of my favorite pastimes is watching Shellye and our girls interact. She's got a way about her that brings tears to my eyes. Whatever the activity, Shellye is right beside them. When they are learning their Scripture memory verses, Shellye is there. Already, Ashleigh can quote nine verses of a psalm at a single clip, in part because Shellye is so supportive. As a mom, she is dedicated to helping both our daughters succeed in their endeavors.

Not that being a full-time mom is easy, especially when your husband travels as much as I do. Shellye is the nightly homework helper, the daily taxi, the resident chef, and keeper of all things domestic. Yet she relishes her life. She sincerely enjoys shuttling the girls to and from school and cheerleading practice—and not as a drive-by mother, either. Shellye is very involved at our girls' school and finds ways to contribute and be a blessing to the staff and faculty.

As a life partner, Shellye is my perfect match, emotionally and otherwise. I value her opinion. She is smart, objective, wise, and knows me better than anybody else does. When questions arise as to the direction of ministry or the choice of songs for an album or which producer or record company is right, I know I can go to Shellye for straightforward, reliable input.

Being transparent and at ease in our conversation is something we have been able to do since that first day in Rosine. There are no egos in the way. We just keep it simple and honest. That freedom allows us to grow individually and as a couple. After a two-and-one-half-hour concert, Shellye will say, "Honey, that set was too long." I don't try to convince her that a one-hundred-fifty-minute concert is a great idea. I take my wife's advice seriously; I know she has my best interests at heart. At the same time, she knows I trust her and won't be offended by the truth. In the end, if you can't tell each other the truth, you have to wonder how solid your relationship really is.

One of the reasons Shellye and I came together in the first place has to do with transparency. At the very beginning, it was clear that Shellye loved me for who I was and not what I did. It wasn't about the music, the recognition, or anything like that. In fact, when we first fell in love, she didn't know the extent of my musical and ministry life.

Shellye liked me as I was. As a result, she brought out the best in me. I had experienced relationships that lacked that kind of truth. In school, everyone had their *crush* and their reasons. I was a country kid with no fancy home or cars or anything to draw attention to me. I wasn't very popular with the girls. In fact, they usually gave me the brush-off. They weren't interested in me—at least, not until I sang at a school variety show. Then, all of a sudden, the girls noticed me. Suddenly, I was in demand.

> *He who finds a wife finds what is good*
> *and receives favor from the LORD.*
> —PROVERBS 18:22

Shellye did not operate that way. She loved me first and learned about what I did afterward. We were blessed in that when we started our relationship, we truly loved each other. We weren't drawn by illusions or impressions or any other distractions. That has proved to be a good foundation for the rest of our life together.

SHELLYE'S TESTIMONY: IT'S NOT ABOUT ME

I met Jason in Rosine, Kentucky, when I was sixteen years old. In all of Kentucky, I may have been the only person who hadn't heard of the Crabb Family. All I knew was that my stepmom and my father were taking me to a concert. There was a guy there my stepmom wanted me to meet.

Moments after I met Jason, he asked me, "What are you doing tonight?"

I said, "I'm going to church."

Without the slightest hesitation, he said, "I'm going with you"—which he did!

That is where our relationship began. We hit it off from the start, but since we lived seventeen miles apart, it wasn't easy getting to see one another. Not only that, but Jason was on the road a lot. Often he would come in during the middle of the week, wake up at six in the morning, and drive over to Central City, where I lived. He would take me to school and return in the evening to pick me up and take me home.

Just about every time Jason came to get me, I would ask him, "What should we do tonight?"

Jason's answer was always the same: "We've got to put up posters."

The posters let everyone know when the Crabb Family would be singing. Once each month, they gave a concert in Owensboro, Kentucky. It took lots of posters to get the word out. That is how we spent most of our dates. And since the Owensboro concerts happened every month, we were never done hanging posters.

Jason and I dated for three years. In 1997, I graduated from high school, and on May 12, 1998, Jason and I got married in my home church. I was nineteen, and he was twenty-one. Our backgrounds were very similar; my parents divorced when I was only four years old, and my dad raised me; my twin sister, Kellye; and our older sister, Leslie.

Because my dad worked on the railroad and was gone a lot of the time, my grandmother lived with us and cared for us kids. She was very involved with my sisters and me and played a very significant role in our lives. So did Dad. He worked really hard to make a living for all of us. My dad and grandmother did a great job raising us—and they made sure we were in church every time the doors opened!

After two years of marriage, Jason and I learned that I was pregnant. We were scared, yet excited. Starting a family was something we both wanted very much. But almost as soon as our dream was underway, it was threatened. Early in the pregnancy, I started having complications. Soon afterward, I had a miscarriage. Jason and I were devastated to lose our baby. We couldn't understand why this had happened to us.

About a year and a half later, I got pregnant again. Our hopes were high, but we lost that baby too. It hit us hard. I remember asking the Lord over and over again to give me the strength to get through the ordeal. He did.

Yet getting through the miscarriages was only part of the process. For so long I struggled with the loss of our babies and the disappointment that followed. At times I almost questioned God; I wanted to ask Him why He allowed everyone but us to have babies. The loss of our children did not make sense to me. Still, I kept praying. At some point I realized that my focus was centered on me and what I wanted. I was preoccupied with the way I thought things should turn out. What I really needed was to get to the point where it wasn't about me.

Through prayer and dedication, I eventually got to where I needed to be. It wasn't about us anymore. It was about what God wanted for our lives. The day came when I could agree with the psalmist who said, "Not to us, O LORD, not to us but to your name be the glory, because of your love and faithfulness" (Ps. 115:1).

Emotionally and spiritually, the change in perspective was dramatic. It not only kept us grounded in our trust of the Lord, but it also helped Jason and me to mature. Needless to say, our growth in this area was not easy; we were being stretched and tested. When you are in a situation like we were in, you sometimes wonder whether it will ever end.

Then one day, God spoke to me! He promised me a child. His promise did not come about right away, yet I knew I had heard His voice. And I knew He was faithful.

SHELLYE'S TESTIMONY: LOOK TO THE FUTURE

When Jason is onstage, he often tells the story of an evangelist friend who told us to buy a box of Pampers—*before* we had even conceived. The man's name is Jay Boyd. Jason has known him since childhood when Jason and his family attended Jay's revival meetings. Jason played drums for Jay at some point, and they have kept in touch over the years. The way Jason tells it, Jay could preach wallpaper right off the walls. I don't doubt it. Jay is fearless about saying whatever he believes God wants said.

We bought that box of Pampers. Every day it served as a reminder that our promise was on its way. It was a tangible symbol of God's promise and involvement in our lives, much as the watch from Pastor Parsley is symbolic of God's faithfulness in Jason's transition to solo ministry.

This pastor encouraged us to be proactive in our faith, thanking God in advance for the blessing of our children. Doing that forced us to take our focus off the past. Jason and I set our sights on what was yet to come. Before six months went by, I was pregnant again! This time, I knew everything was going to be fine. In fact, there was not a single doubt in my mind. I just started thanking God for our baby, knowing that He was taking care of us.

He was and still is taking care of us—all four of us! Now, when I look back to the years before the births of Ashleigh Taylor and Emmaleigh Love, I understand why things happened the way they did. The Lord has shown me, and continues to show me, the good that came out of our trial. Night after night, women with similar heartaches come to our table. They are hurting and wondering *why,* just as we were during those hard years. Now we have precious opportunities to minister to them. And because we walked through the same flames, these women realize that they can come through the fire too.

God is faithful. He will comfort others as He comforted us! He will help others to understand the things He helped us to understand. They too will come out of the fire knowing that "…neither death nor life, neither angels nor demons, neither the present nor the future, nor any powers, neither height nor depth, nor anything else in all creation, will be able to separate us from the love of God that is in Christ Jesus our Lord" (Rom. 8:38–39). In His wisdom and because of our experiences, God has given us a special way to share His love.

There is one other thing God showed me after our trial ended. I learned that trials are often one part *why* and an equal part *when*. It is clear to me now that when Jason and I first conceived, it was not the right time for us. The first five years of our marriage helped us to draw close and build a stronger bond between us. God had something in mind for that season, and it wasn't children.

"For I know the plans I have for you," declares the LORD, *"plans to prosper you and not to harm you, plans to give you hope and a future."*

—JEREMIAH 29:11

GOD IS FAITHFUL

Through the struggle, we continued to minister. At times, when Shellye and I were on the bus, I'd look over at her and see tears in her eyes. Those tears did the talking even when no words were exchanged.

There was a question in my wife's tears. The question was, "Why?" To this day, I really can't say why Shellye and I endured the devastation of miscarriages. At this point, I'm not sure I need to know. I do know this: our experiences have helped us to bless others. So many people suffer the heartbreak of losing a baby. The numbers are staggering. In fact, depending upon the statistical source, as many as one out of four women suffer a miscarriage.

There are a lot of hurting people behind those numbers. For Shellye and me, it is easy to relate to them. We know what it is like to lose a child. It is hard—really hard. Yet even in the midst of our losses, we were not without hope. Nor was I without a voice. I just kept singing "Through the Fire" and "Still Holding On." I knew I could trust God to show up and carry me past the pain again.

Those two songs encouraged Shellye and me when we needed it most. It was as though God was saying, "I am faithful, and I will continue to be faithful." He was giving us, through whatever means necessary, the strength to heed the words David wrote during his own desperate times: "Be strong and take heart, all you who hope in the LORD" (Ps. 31:24).

God used those songs to renew our hope and refresh our souls. He used people too. Shellye told you about Jay Boyd and the Pampers. Jay knew my family for years. His and my dad's relationship dated back before the Crabb Family Singers to the days when my dad was a minister. I remember Jay in the pulpit—the man could preach! I am thankful that our relationship has continued throughout the years.

Jay told Shellye and me to thank God for the promise *before* it came to pass. He said we needed to do what the Bible says and call "things that are not as though they were" (Rom. 4:17). We needed to be like the men who tore the roof off a building because they believed Jesus would heal the paralyzed man they brought to Him (Mark 2:1–12). We needed to be like Jairus trusting Jesus, even in the worst circumstances (Mark 5:22–43). We needed to come to the place where no matter the setbacks we would remain focused on the love and power of God to bless and heal.

All of Christianity is built on that kind of faith. It is the faith that says, "When doubt comes, we'll praise Him. When life comes apart at the seams, we'll praise Him. No matter the outcome, we'll praise Him. Whether the promise comes to pass or it doesn't, we'll praise Him."

That last one is a tough nut to crack. It means selling out to God to such a degree that your dreams are not as important as the fact that you are His. It took Shellye and me time to get there. We were not satisfied with the outcome of two miscarriages. We were not satisfied to be childless. I won't kid you; after the second miscarriage, I threw my hands in the air and said, "God, I may not be the greatest father, but I will be a grateful father."

In the midst of an ordeal like that, there are moments when you feel hopeless and unable to push past the sorrow. We often minister to people who feel exactly that way. Our hearts break for them, because we understand. We are so privileged to pray for them. How blessed we are to hear their testimonies afterward! Some of them write us to say that they have given birth. Others are ecstatic when they tell us that God answered their prayers through adoption. Still, I know that some of them have yet to see their dreams fulfilled.

For those who have had miscarriages, there is good news: your babies are in heaven. So are our babies. As hard as it was to lose them, I get excited to think that someday Ashleigh and Emmaleigh will meet their siblings in heaven!

At some distant day, all six of us will be there together.

WHY, GOD?

It is not easy to *be strong and take heart* when things happen in defiance of God's promises. In those crushing moments, it is hard to know what to think or how to respond. Should we trust in silence and ignore our doubts? Or should we deny our emotions, as though we were not in turmoil?

Our responses to difficulty have a lot to do with how we were raised and what we have been told about God. Some people say we should never, *ever* question God. Yet some of the greatest leaders and prophets in all of history have asked Him tough questions.

When Abraham learned of God's plan to *investigate* the sin of Sodom and Gomorrah, Abraham pressed God to share His intentions. He wanted to know whether God would kill his nephew Lot and Lot's family along with the depraved. Abraham asked God point-blank, "Will you sweep away the righteous with the wicked?" (Gen. 18:23). He continued to press God until God assured him that the handful of righteous people living in the forsaken place would be spared (Gen. 18:24–32).

Life is full of questions. Not all of them are as pressing as our questions about death, suffering, and loss. Yet, even if we had never experienced a day of adversity, we would ask our Father the curious questions children always ask their parents:

- "How many stars are in the sky?"
- "Why is grass green?"
- "Why do we park in the driveway and drive on the parkway?"

- "Why is my last name Crabb?" (Imagine how much adversity a name like that can generate at school!)
- "Why...what...how...when...where?"

My point is this: if you have taken oxygen into your lungs, you know that life is marked by trials and heartaches. We experience circumstances we don't understand and don't want to embrace. We have questions and will continue to have questions as long as we are breathing, and maybe even after that. Who is better able to answer us than God? He wasn't surprised by Abraham's questions, and He won't be surprised by ours.

I have met people in all kinds of situations. Often I can almost hear their hearts asking, "Why, God?" Recently I prayed with a woman in the Midwest. She wanted me to ask God to help her keep her new job. She said, "I have an incurable disease."

She lost her health insurance when she took the new job. That sounds like trouble enough for someone with an incurable disease. Yet she feared something worse. She feared being without work. She had a family to support and was worried about getting fired. I got the sense that she was a single parent. Whatever her status, she was obviously under a lot of pressure and had decided to make choices designed to improve her lot. She believed her new job would open a fresh chapter in her life.

She summed up her thoughts by saying something unforgettable: "I have to get back to living."

As the tears streamed down her cheeks, I started praying for words of encouragement, something God would have her hear. In my mind, I imagined the questions piercing her heart.

"Am I going to make it?"

"Will I lose my job?"

"Am I going to die?"

"Will they find a cure for this disease, or will God heal me?"

Then I asked this dear woman a question: "Do you believe that God can heal you?"

"I am trying to," she said. "I'm going to church and hanging on to every word the preacher says."

Although her unanswered questions lingered, I knew she would be all right when she said, "I have to get back to living." Her life had been as tough as nails, but she was not about to give up. Nor was she willing to accept the bleak picture the devil was trying to present to her.

We must never forget that the devil is a liar. Lying is his stock and trade. Therefore it is up to us to take the offense where he and his lies are concerned. When he tempts me, I like to ask myself this question: What if Satan had to tell the truth about himself, about God, and about our destinies? What kind of picture would he paint then? How successful would he be at killing, stealing, and destroying lives if he could suggest nothing but truth?

The answer is that he would fail miserably at deceiving us. Unfortunately, truth is not the enemy's hallmark. He continues to seek those "he may devour" (1 Pet. 5:8, KJV.) The sense I got from the woman who wanted to get back to living was that she refused to be devoured by a liar. She was determined to keep moving forward. I like to see that kind of tenacity. People like her are hard to forget. In fact, I will never forget her or that altar service.

There are so many memories like that. The people we meet touch our hearts as much as we do theirs, if not more. I remember an outdoor concert from some years ago, before "Through the Fire" was completed. In fact, at the time, Dad had only part of the song worked out. He had started it at the piano, but after a year, he was still stuck; the rest of the song just wouldn't come together.

We had a product table at the concert. On that particular day, Dad was behind the table, and I was standing nearby. A woman walked up to Dad with a child in her arms. The woman asked Dad, "When you get back on the bus, will you pray for me? My son needs an operation, and my husband just left me." We prayed for her right there.

A prayer request like that can take your breath away. Yet this woman showed great strength; as she turned to walk away, she reminded us about faith's bottom line. Her last words to us were, "I'm still trusting in the Lord that He's going to help me through all this."

Her parting words were as riveting as her prayer request. We were reminded once again that there is always someone who is going through something worse than what we are experiencing. God used her to put our lives and issues into clear perspective.

That night Dad wrote the rest of "Through the Fire."

CHAPTER 2

FACING WEAKNESS AND FRUSTRATION

Many times in trials,
weakness blurs my vision

And my frustration
gets so out of hand.

STRENGTHENED BY OTHERS

WHATEVER YOUR CALLING in life, whatever your family situation, you have experienced daunting days in which all the strength you could muster was not enough.

You are not alone. There are days when all my strength seems like no strength at all. At times, my cup overflows with nothing but weakness. It doesn't matter how I felt or how I saw myself the day before; it may have seemed like I was sitting on top of the world. Yet something happens or something is said, and it rocks my world. That's when I need someone—Shellye, my parents, *someone*—to give me a loving but firm reality check and say, "Welcome to the real world."

By God's grace I have learned some things along the way. For one, I realize that the challenges we face have a mind of their own. They don't ask permission to enter our lives, and they don't wait in line until we feel ready to deal with them. They typically rush in without warning—not one at a time but in a flood.

That is when my weaknesses are most apparent, and my switches can get flipped. My first reaction usually runs along these lines: "Why now? Why me? Where did this come from?" If I continue in that mind-set, I dig myself a deeper hole until weakness isn't my only problem. Something else rushes out from behind the curtain of my emotions. That something is frustration.

Merriam-Webster defines *frustration* as "the state or an instance of being frustrated...a deep chronic sense or state of insecurity and dissatisfaction arising from unresolved problems or unfulfilled needs."[1] Listen to the words associated with frustration:

chronic . . . insecurity . . . dissatisfaction . . . unresolved . . . unfulfilled.
Frustration is a heavy load to carry!

I have dragged that load around more than once. The longer I choose to remain shackled to it, the heavier the burden becomes. The sense of weakness that created the frustration in the first place grows more intense. It is a vicious cycle. the weaker I feel, the more frustrated I get; the more frustrated I get, the weaker I feel. My perspective narrows. My thoughts become overly centered on self— my fears, my abilities, my needs, and my expectations. Pretty soon, self-pity moves in and tries to eat me alive.

No wonder God puts other people in our lives! We can relate to one another's pain and help each other walk through the fire. I have seen my family do it many times. Just being close to other people helps me to remember that what I am experiencing is not as unusual or surprising as it feels. First Corinthians 10:13 says, *"No* temptation has seized you except what is *common* to man" (emphasis added).

There are always others who have walked through the fire before us. Their testimonies, examples, and guidance give us strength. I am thankful for those who have gone before me in gospel music. Amazing people have become my mentors and have affected my development by their examples. Not all of them are friends; some have mentored me without even knowing it. Others are personally involved in my life. I could never put a price on the inspiration these leaders provide. What I can say is that I take their gifts, experiences, and wisdom to heart. Their input strengthens my faith and bolsters my ministry and professional foundation. They are willing to share the lessons they have learned, which allows me to build upon those lessons.

In the area of mentors, I have been more than doubly blessed. For so many years, my dad was literally within arm's reach. All that time, he was the twenty-four-hour-per-day, seven-days-per-week mentor who taught me more about music and ministry than I can begin to tell.

Everything Dad did musically was done from his desire to serve God. It still is. His input was constant and spanned all the phases of my growth as a singer and musician. I have already shared one of my earliest memories as a songwriter; it was the time Dad cheered me on and recorded my voice singing lyrics I had written about Jesus. There was a later period in my youth when I became more focused on playing drums and bass than on singing. Dad flowed right with me. He and I burned the midnight oil, stoking my passion in a way that taught me not only musical lessons but life lessons.

If Dad had been my only mentor, it would have been enough. Yet I have also been privileged to be mentored by the great Bill Gaither. Talk about an example! Bill was formally trained as a teacher. He loves doing it. You need only spend a few minutes in Bill's company talking about gospel music or discussing direction for your life, and you find yourself learning things that never would have occurred to you except for that conversation.

During a transition period for the Gaither Vocal Band, I got to travel with Bill and fill in as a singer for the group. It was an unforgettable experience. Bill's expertise cannot be measured. He knows how to do a concert right. He is a master at everything from songwriting to set lists to worship and sound. It would take a chapter to list his professional accomplishments. Bill has received countless awards and commendations over the years. One that almost captures the breadth of his impact was an award given Bill and his wife, Gloria, in the year 2000. They were named "Gospel Songwriters of the Century" by the American Society of Composers and Performers (ASCAP)![2]

There is no doubt: my grandkids will be listening to the Gaithers' songs in decades to come! Yet, far beyond his achievements, Bill is an outstanding man of God and a huge part of my life. He is someone whose example I can trust and am humbled to follow.

Other people have left their imprint upon my life. When I was fifteen or sixteen years old, I attended the annual National Quartet Convention, one of Southern Gospel music's main events for more than six decades. The Gaither Vocal Band was performing at the convention that year with Michael English leading the vocals. The sound of his voice stopped me dead in my tracks. It connected with my soul because the music came straight from his. Songs like "Satisfied" and "I Bowed on My Knees and Cried Holy" got me absolutely hooked on the music.

That soul-to-soul connection is the key to a great song. It is something my dad knows a lot about. His songs have had that quality from the very beginning. I asked him one day, "Dad, how do you write these songs?"

He answered, "Son, to write them, you've got to live them. You have to go through some fires before you can talk about the heat."

Some of Dad's best songs were written from a place of weakness and frustration. They flowed from his soul when his head was jammed with the difficulties and trials of life. Before recording my debut solo album, I called my dad. When he picked up the phone, I asked him how he was doing.

"I'm having a hard day, son," Dad replied.

We talked a little about what he was going through and went on to other things. Three days later, Dad called me with a new song called "Sometimes I Cry." The song was birthed from the pain he was in. The chorus tells the story better than I can:

> But sometimes I hurt and sometimes I cry
> Sometimes I can't get it right
> No matter how hard I try
> Sometimes I fall down
> Stumble over my own disguise
> I try to look strong
> As the whole world looks on
> But sometimes alone I cry.[3]

When you hear a song like that, you know instantly that it's a living, breathing piece of the person who wrote it. When you sing it, you connect with the song and your audience in ways that God can use to bring healing. I ended up recording "Sometimes I Cry" on the record that was just getting underway. It is the most frequently downloaded cut from the album.

That kind of authenticity inspires me. It reminds me that weakness and frustration are part of life. We needn't surrender to them, but we have to acknowledge them in order to move on with God. My mentors have taught me that lesson not only by their words but also through their actions. They inspire me to press through difficulties, extract from them something of value, and share that something with others.

PRACTICE, PRACTICE, PRACTICE

You eventually reach an age where young, aspiring musicians seek your advice. These future gospel music artists usually ask me how they can get started. I tell them, "Practice, practice, practice, and leave the rest to God's timing." I explain that God has got to be the One in control and motivating the pursuit. Once that foundation is established, it is our job to cooperate with Him by developing our gifts.

It may sound trite, but it's true: you have to know two things before you choose a life in gospel music. First, you have to understand that your gifts come from God. Second, you have to know that He has called you to gospel music. The rest of the learning comes as you walk out the calling. I always recommend listening to favorite singers. You can absorb a lot of information when you hear the music that inspires you. But, as I always tell gospel music hopefuls, "Before you quit your day job, make sure you spend time in the Word and in prayer, because this is not a life of glamour."

Ministry is not all fun. It is a demanding life. I'm certain that if I invited a busload of young musicians to travel with me for a week, some of them would have a change of heart. The rigors of the road are formidable. Many of the people who couldn't wait to get on the bus might be even more eager to jump off! The tamer lifestyle awaiting them at home could seem a whole lot more attractive than it once did.

Life on the road is a life of extremes. When you are traveling, you go through rapid-fire highs and lows. After a mind-blowing concert, you still have to climb into a small bunk on a moving bus. I think about my wife and kids and the cheerleading event I missed or the night we could have spent in front of the fireplace together. There are natural swings of passion and frustration, elation and weariness. We see God do amazing things, but there is no getting around the price.

I don't mean to make it sound like drudgery. It's not. I would not trade my life for any other. But the fact remains that the intensity can cut both ways. So when someone asks, "How can I get started in gospel music?" I swallow hard and try to answer as honestly as I possibly can. I'm not looking to play God with anyone's hopes and dreams. All I have is my own experience, and from it I can tell you this: if you are prepared to deal with the downside of a ministry in gospel music, the upside is *amazing*.

LAUGHTER IS GOOD MEDICINE

There is a serious side to gospel music, but that's only part of the picture. There is a certain amount of hilarity involved when you travel from city to city for days or weeks at a clip. Some experiences don't seem funny at the time, especially when they happen on stage or in a church.

The truth is, some of the craziest things happen in church services. One night, which happened to be my birthday, we had anything but a party going on. Whatever could go wrong did go wrong. The sound system kept cutting in and out while we were singing. Then, when the music was done (which was probably a relief for the audience!) we turned to leave the platform. As Kelly walked down the steps leading off the stage, she lost her footing and tumbled down the steep incline. Thankfully, she didn't fall headfirst or suffer any serious injuries. Still, the distraction of someone going thump...

thump...thump down the ramp was jarring. It was going to be difficult to finish the service. Kelly was shaken up enough to say, "I'm not going back on that stage." However, after some persuasive parenting from our folks, she did.

After all of the calamity, we loaded up the bus feeling like we had done a terrible job. Every flaw and shortcoming was magnified. Frustration was thick in the air. Like anyone who has had a bad day, we had to deal with the fallout of failure. In our case, we felt that we had failed our audience.

Before we dug ourselves a hole too deep, the bigger picture came back into focus. The only way to put the night into proper perspective was to circle back to this truth: none of what we do is about us or about our performance. It is always about what *He* has in mind and what *He* is doing. That doesn't mean that we don't try our best. It just means that we have to trust in God both when things are going great and when our best efforts fail.

May the God of hope fill you with all joy and peace as you trust in him, so that you may overflow with hope by the power of the Holy Spirit.
—ROMANS 15:13

It is amazing how God restores our joy and peace when we need it most. He always loves us and is always aware of what concerns us. That night on the bus, after what looked like a train wreck of a service, He reassured us that the night's mishaps were not the big deal we imagined. We learned that when things go haywire, the best response is to laugh at yourself and remember that every day and every church service is different—and some are *really* different.

Church isn't the only place where crazy things happen. We have had our share of bloopers and frustrations on the bus too. One time, while en route to a church service, the air conditioning went out. It was a scorcher of a day, and the bus heated up in a hurry. By the time we got to the church, we were desperate to cool off.

Our hopes of air-conditioned relief died quickly when the power in the church went out. Air conditioning was the least of our problems; without power, we were about to hold what would amount to a silent worship service—in the dark. Talk about feeling helpless!

Then it occurred to us: the bus had no air conditioning, but it still had power. We ran a cable from the bus to the church and kept the service going by way of the generator. The bus produced enough electricity for the sound system and lights, but the heat was still oppressive. By the end of the service, we were soaked in sweat. It was going to be a long night on the bus. Then Kathy grabbed a garden hose and turned it on us. What a relief it was, and what fun we had! We were like a bunch of kids frolicking under a sprinkler in the front yard.

It was the perfect ending to a long, hard day. When we got back on the bus, it was still 98 degrees, but we were cool. Soaking wet, but cool.

There is a time for everything, and a season for every activity under heaven....a time to weep and a time to laugh....

—Ecclesiastes 3:1, 4

The Birthing Stage

You have already heard about our days licking envelopes, putting up posters, and driving a bus whose days were numbered. Some of our routine tasks have changed over the years, but one thing is still true: what happens onstage is only part of the story. There is always a lot more that goes on behind the scenes. Most of it is *good ol'* hard work. People rarely see what happens off the stage, but without it, concerts just wouldn't happen.

When I first started singing and ministering with my family, we had to *minister* to our bus on a regular basis. Whether engine work or generator repairs were needed, we were the mechanics on call. Living on the road so much of the time meant piling on the mileage. There was no avoiding frequent repairs and maintenance.

One maintenance routine sticks out in my mind. Every so often, we had to get under the bus and grease it. We didn't have the right equipment to do the job; we just crawled under the bus and did the best we could with what we had. We never failed to come out from under the bus completely blackened from head to toe. It was a mess. Getting the grease off our bodies and out of our clothes was a routine of its own.

It sounds like a funny scene, and, truth be told, we had some laughs fixing the bus; but *fun* is not the word that comes to mind when I think of all the time we spent doing it. Engines, oil changes, or grease guns seem to be a far cry from gospel singing; yet, those chores had everything to do with fulfilling God's call on our family. His mandate is never a call to the limelight, glamour, or ease. It is not a call to a predictable, neatly arranged life either. In our experience, it has always been more of an ongoing work in progress.

Like all the amazing things God does, the circumstances surrounding our work rarely seem perfect. This was true when we started out, and it is true now. There have been many days when my family and I felt as though nothing were under our control. As frustrating as that can be at times, it is actually an accurate assessment of the reality.

Everything is under *His* control. If we can just accept that, we will always see ourselves as being blessed—weak and frustrated, maybe, but blessed. Looking back, we have been. He has always been there to take us by the hand and walk us through the fire, one day at a time.

Your beginnings will seem humble, so prosperous will your future be.

—JOB 8:7

BIRTHING REVISITED

After more than fifteen years on the road as a ministry family, you get some of the kinks worked out, and you find a certain degree of comfort in what you are doing. Life on the road is never predictable, but after years on the learning curve, you get better at handling the surprises. Once you figure out how to use your bus to generate electricity for a church service, a power outage doesn't seem like the end of the world. If a pastor calls to say, "We are having a blackout. We can't hold service tonight," you don't get wrapped around the axle over it; you can stay calm and offer a solution.

That said, you never really *arrive* in any area of life. You reach plateaus, but they always lead to new jumping-off points. No matter how long you've been doing something, the status quo never lasts. While we gained confidence in certain areas, circumstances highlighted our weakness in others. When our parents quit touring with us, my siblings and I felt less secure than we had all those years. We knew we were going to have to take on new responsibilities and make the decisions that had been made for us in the past.

I can't speak for my brothers and sisters, but I can tell you that there were days I wished my folks would change their minds. As the oldest of the Crabb children on tour, I wondered whether I had what it would take to step it up. I knew what to do, but I had yet to be tested doing it without my parents at my side.

You don't have to live very long to realize that we humans are fallible, prone to worry, touched by fear, and aware of our weaknesses. When the rug is pulled out from under us by a job change, a death, a marital failure, or an illness, we can have knee-jerk reactions. Typically, the first reaction is to resist the change. It is as though our default position is to expect things to go from bad to worse. We find it hard to imagine that *any* good could come out of a new situation. So, rather than risk failure, we stamp the mission *impossible*. We accept defeat before it happens and are done with it.

The second reaction is to shift into overdrive and then power our way through the challenges. We forget that we have a Savior, and we try to save ourselves (and everyone else in the process). We trick ourselves into believing that sheer muscle will ensure success, but in reality, we set ourselves up for defeat and disappointment.

I told you about my misgivings before going solo. There were so many hurdles within my own heart, not the least of which was the overriding fear that I would fall flat on my face. A solo move would force my reentry into the birthing process; there was no getting around that. There were leadership concerns too. I would have to stand on my own two feet and face my weaknesses head-on. It didn't look pretty from where I was standing. In fact, I was a nervous wreck at first. I was being stretched, big-time.

The apostle Paul obviously had a similar experience during a time of great weakness. He appealed to God to remove the tormenting thorn from his flesh. (See 2 Corinthians 12:7–8.) Christ responded to Paul saying, "My grace is sufficient for you, for my power is made perfect in weakness" (2 Cor. 12:9). I knew those words were as true for me as they were for Paul. Yet, I also knew that I was about to enter uncharted territory. I would have to trust Him in ways I knew nothing about. There would have to be some growth in me; I would have to go through some fresh fire before I could "…boast all the more gladly about my weaknesses, so that Christ's power [might] rest on me" (2 Cor. 12:9).

A RETURN TO GOD

At every point along the way, through thick and thin, God encouraged my family and me and made a way for us to do His will. One of the wonderful surprises that delights me to this day involves Norm Livingston, a renowned gospel music promoter, and the Paynes, a gospel group known for smash hit songs like "Out of This World" and "Rapture."

The Paynes did a famous live album entitled *Fire on Stage*. It was recorded on the stage of Dayton Memorial Hall in Dayton, Ohio. The record became a Crabb family favorite. We listened to it over and over again, often while traveling. It is an album you cannot help but be affected by, not only because the music gets inside you but also because Mike Payne's lyrics are so powerful.

I can still remember how the album started out with the voice of Norm Livingston introducing the group. The sound of it never failed to thrill me. If you had told me in those early years that Norm Livingston would introduce a Crabb Family live recording in the future and that we would play on the stage of Dayton Memorial Hall, I would have told you to think again. But I was wrong.

Norm would eventually promote Crabb Family events. One concert was recorded for a live album and—you guessed it—Norm introduced us, just as he had introduced yhe Paynes years before! It was another one of those milestones, a moment in time when God gave the Crabb Family His stamp of approval. Not only that, but he blessed us with the friendship of Norm Livingston. I can't tell you how it increased my faith.

One night, after another concert promoted by Norm Livingston, a dear friend who is a powerful man of God and pastor of the Vandalia Christian Tabernacle, Todd Hoskins, talked with me while I rolled some sound cable. Just then a woman walked up to us. She was crying; it was obvious that her heart was broken. She told us about her backslidden husband and shared about how he had once served the Lord. Every time the church doors were open, he was there—even at prayer meetings. He attended all the revivals, and if anything needed to be done, he volunteered to do it. Then something happened. He turned to drugs and alcohol and withdrew from the Lord. She didn't even know where he was.

With tears streaming down her face and her crying son in her arms, the distraught woman said, "All I want you to do is pray for my husband when you get on the bus." It was late, and we still had work to do. At the end of the night, it can be hard to push past the exhaustion, but I knew God wanted us to stop and help this woman. I jumped off the stage and said, "Let's pray right now."

Looking from the natural perspective, this woman's situation was beyond any of us. Her husband was a grown-up with a mind of his own. He could have resisted God for the rest of his life if he wanted to. Besides, I know I am just a man myself. I have to look in the mirror every day and face the fact that I too have missed the mark.

Yet I also know that God gave us a mission. He would not call us to do it and withhold the help needed to accomplish it. Jesus said to "go into all the world and preach the good news to all creation" (Mark 16:15). The Bible says, "The prayer of a righteous man is powerful and effective" (James 5:16). Sometimes that is all we need to know.

Todd Hoskins and I prayed with this dear woman. As we did, we knew the Lord was doing something special. We prayed for her husband knowing that God knew exactly where he was and what kind of help he needed. We prayed, "God, convict his heart—no matter where he is."

Before we closed with an *amen*, the woman's pastor walked up to us. When he saw that she was upset, he followed her back into the concert hall. He stood off at a distance as she told us about her prayer request, and he prayed with us from where he was standing. As soon as we were finished, his cell phone rang.

The call was from the woman's husband. He was crying and said, "Pastor, I really need you to come over to the house. I've been running from God. I've run as long as I can, and I need to get right with Him. So as soon as you get home, please come over and let's pray."

As soon as I learned who was on the phone, I had to repent. Although we had prayed believing for God to move, I was shocked to see Him move so quickly! It blew my mind that He had spoken to someone who wasn't there with us, someone we could not have even found.

Not only was the woman elated, but also all of us felt stronger in our faith because of the experience we shared. More importantly, a child of the King, a husband, and a father wanted to come back to God and back to his loved ones.

Everyone who believes in him receives forgiveness of sins through his name.

—ACTS 10:43

THE REAL THING

When you come right down to it, there are two basic approaches to dealing with the weaknesses and frustration we experience: we can try to paper over our shortcomings and deny that we struggle at times, or we can choose to be transparent, own up to our failings, and allow God to cleanse us.

Whether or not you live in the public eye, it can be hard to come out from behind the façades. We all have them. We erect them because we all feel vulnerable in some way. Yet, when we choose to hold on to our *stuff* and then seek ways to hide it, we imprison ourselves behind these façades. The trouble is, they are hard to create and even harder to protect.

Hiding wastes precious energy and resources; it also causes us to squander valuable opportunities to help others. When I called my dad a few days before he wrote "Sometimes I Cry," he could have avoided my question and said that he was doing fine. The façade would have given him cover and allowed him to appear stronger than he was. It would also have closed the door on divine opportunities. By stuffing his emotions, he would have missed out on an important step in his personal growth. The chances are also good that "Sometimes I Cry" would not have been written.

A dear pastor friend of mine once told me, "Never be scared to talk about what has happened in your life." I took his words to heart. It is part of what motivates me as I share my own story.

We are all weak and prone to being frustrated. Every one of us has suffered pain. The only thing that will come from hiding our struggles is more weakness, frustration, and pain. If, on the other hand, we are willing to come down to earth and be ourselves, we can do some heavenly good here on the earth.

For Christ's sake, I delight in weaknesses, in insults, in hardships, in persecutions, in difficulties. For when I am weak, then I am strong.

—2 CORINTHIANS 12:10

CHAPTER 3

FEELING ALL ALONE

It's then I am reminded
I've never been forsaken

And I've never had to
stand the test alone.

GOD'S ANSWER TO *ALONE*

The life of faith is an adventure. It is rewarding, exciting, and pleasing to God. Yet it has its challenges. There are moments when it feels as though you are walking through the fire alone. On those days when the battle is fierce, your mind will tell you it's all over, even as God is telling you to forge ahead.

When I stepped out into solo ministry, I honestly felt as though I were about to walk off the edge of the earth—by myself and without a net! Those were difficult days in ministry, a season of being nearly overwhelmed with all that needed to be done. Frankly, it was more than Shellye and I could do on our own. Beyond the sheer logistics of the thing, we knew little about the business side of establishing a new ministry and creating a sound financial structure to support it.

I didn't feel at all prepared for such a big step, but I knew God had called me to take it. What I didn't realize was that He had already made provision for our needs. In fact, He had set the wheels of provision in motion eight years earlier when he brought Philip and Tina Morris into our lives.

Philip heard "Please Forgive Me" on the radio and learned that the Crabb Family Singers were coming to a town near where he and Tina lived. They ended up coming to a number of our concerts and bought a CD at one of them. Philip learned from the liner notes that my idea of a favorite day off was one spent in a deer stand. The next time Philip came to a concert, he asked me where I liked to hunt. I explained that I didn't have a really good place to hunt anymore. Philip had a great place to hunt. He invited me; Shellye;

my sister Terah; and her husband, Jonathan, to spend a few days on a large tract of his land to do some hunting.

Philip and Tina became part of our family. The four of us hunted and took trips together, and we invited them to many of our events. In the summertime, Philip took us boating. He and Tina were there when our girls were born and through my transition from the Crabb Family to solo ministry.

Philip and Tina are professional people. When we met, Philip was an executive in manufacturing and had been in the field some thirty years. Tina had been in banking for almost two decades. (She now works in higher education.)

When the Crabb family's joint ministry came to an end, Philip and Tina helped us to get the business details and finances worked out. Whatever needed to be done, they helped do it. That included setting up and maintaining our payroll and making sure the ministry's bills were paid. They still worked their own careers full-time, so whatever Philip and Tina did for us, they did at night. I know they burned the midnight oil to help me, yet they wouldn't take a dime for their efforts. They were Jesus with skin on—a manifestation of God's goodness and provision when I needed it most.

Not long ago, Philip left manufacturing to work with me full-time. I know it was a big step. To tell you the truth, it scared me to think about all he was giving up for the ministry. Yet he felt God had been preparing him all his life for such a time as this. His expertise in business, finance, and contracts—everything he had learned over thirty-eight years—made him the perfect manager for this gospel music singer!

The Morrises make it possible for me to be on the road week-in and week-out. They lift the burdens I cannot carry when I am out there singing and preaching and praying with folks. And Tina, who is still serving as the full-time vice president and dean of a local college, continues to keep our books and see to it that our bills are paid!

If you asked him, I know Philip would talk about how God has blessed him in this venture. There is something about the work we do that keeps us both mindful of the cross and growing bolder in our faith. We make the most wonderful friends all over the country too. It is a very enriching life, without a doubt. Yet, I also know I am the bigger beneficiary in our relationship.

There is no way to really understand or express all that Philip and Tina mean to me. Whenever I give them a Christmas or birthday card, I try to put my love and appreciation into words, but the words fail me every time. There are no words to express how I feel about them. I trust them like almost no one else in the world. In fact, I would trust them with my own wife and kids, even more than I trust myself.

When it looked like I would be alone in solo ministry, God provided Philip and Tina. I cannot imagine my life without their friendship and support.

POSSESS YOUR BLESSINGS

God gives blessings, but He leaves it up to us to possess them. When He spoke to my siblings and me about pursuing separate ministries, He showed us His hand. We knew that if we obeyed Him in faith in spite of our concerns, He would bless us and our efforts. Yet, it wasn't as though we said, "Yes, Lord," and all of our fears faded on the spot. We had to confront the uncertainty and go forward. There would be a battle for the blessing; the fight was in our minds, where it always is.

The Book of Numbers provides a crystal-clear example of the spiritual battle waged in the human mind. Recorded in the thirteenth chapter of the book is the story of Moses and the twelve spies. Moses sent these men to Canaan to search out the land God had promised them. When they returned, Moses asked them to report on how God's chosen place looked.

God had already told Moses a lot about the Promised Land, so I used to wonder why a scouting report was necessary. Today I believe that God's intention was to rally the Israelites. As they drew near Canaan to possess it, He sought to bolster their faith. They had been on the road for years and had often lost focus on the fulfillment of God's promise. They needed a verbal and visual aid to prepare them for their new life.

In today's vocabulary, God was arranging a pep rally! Do you remember having pep rallies at school? In my school, we had them right before the game. A good pep rally would get everyone on the same page—rooting for the team and believing they would *possess* the win. I believe that's what God really wanted to see happen when He sent out the twelve spies.

Yet even when God speaks, we can remain hardwired to old mind-sets. Instead of accepting what God has said, we become intimidated by the details. We fail to line up with God's perspective; therefore we get caught up in doubt and end up feeling defeated, even before our venture has begun.

That is exactly what happened with ten of the twelve spies. When they returned to Moses, they began their report by saying, "Surely the land flows with milk and honey." (See Numbers 13:27.)

That was an understatement! It took two men to carry a single cluster of grapes back from the land. Can you picture grapes that big? Have you ever seen two people working hard to carry a single bunch out of the supermarket? Yet, that is what happened in the Promised Land. Why? Because when God prepares something for His children, He never does it halfway. He does it all the way, even to the point that it exceeds what we are prepared to believe.

BELIEVE THE VOICE OF GOD

Regardless of the size of the grapes, the ten doubt-filled spies added a *but* to their assessment of the Promised Land. They told Moses, "*But* the people who live there are powerful, and the cities are fortified and very large. We even saw descendants of Anak there" (Num. 13:28, emphasis added).

The descendants of Anak were giants. No doubt, they were an intimidating bunch. For sure, they scared ten of the spies, who went on to tell Moses, "We saw the Nephilim there (the descendants of Anak come from the Nephilim). We seemed like grasshoppers in our own eyes, and we looked the same to them" (Num. 13:33).

The ten spies lost heart because the giants were bigger than they were. They were right; physically speaking, the giants were bigger. The flaw in the Israelites' thinking was the notion that the giants were bigger than the voice and promise of God. They forgot who was backing them up. They lost sight of the fact that their enemies—no matter how big—were no match for God.

Instead of questioning their own mind-sets, the ten spies doubted God. Sometimes we do the same thing. All kinds of *giants* pop up in our everyday lives. We need to remember that the yardstick we use to measure our problems is deceiving—nothing is big or bad enough to hamstring God. Deep down, we know this. We know God has more for us. He has a promised place for us, a land He has set aside for us. We know that some way, somehow, we must continue to believe His voice, because everything He says is trustworthy.

The Bible says that whomever the Son sets free is free indeed (John 8:36). Once He has freed us from our sins, nothing and nobody can defeat us. No giant can compete with the power of His blood. Nothing and no one will separate us from His love. *Every giant must flee!*

Who shall separate us from the love of Christ? Shall trouble or hardship or persecution or famine or nakedness or danger or sword?…No, in all these things we are more than conquerors through him who loved us.

—ROMANS 8:35, 37

GOD IS ON YOUR SIDE

Despite the moans and groans of ten worried spies, two others kept their minds on the promise. One of them was Caleb. He would not cut loose of what God had prepared for His people. Caleb was confident of God's faithfulness. He refuted the naysayers and encouraged the Israelites, saying, "We should go up and take possession of the land, for we can certainly do it" (Num. 13:30).

The ten spies remained unconvinced and continued to predict defeat. The effect on the Israelites was so negative that they began to devise a plan to return to Egypt! Caleb and the other faithful spy, Joshua (who would lead Israel after Moses's death), would not be silent.

> Joshua son of Nun and Caleb son of Jephunneh, who were among those who had explored the land, tore their clothes and said to the entire Israelite assembly, "The land we passed through and explored is exceedingly good. If the LORD is pleased with us, he will lead us into that land, a land flowing with milk and honey, and will give it to us. Only do not rebel against the LORD. And do not be afraid of the people of the land, because we will swallow them up. Their protection is gone, but the LORD is with us. Do not be afraid of them."
>
> —NUMBERS 14:6–9

I like what Joshua and Caleb said: "If the LORD is pleased with us, he will lead us into that land." What this means, I believe, is that God has favor on us when we please Him. We please Him by believing what He said and by bringing back a positive report—in other words, by agreeing with what He promised us!

The difference between Joshua and Caleb and the rest of the spies was attitude. A bad attitude can ruin your day, and more. It can destroy your report and, in turn, your testimony. The faithful spies understood this and told their fellow Israelites, "Do not rebel against the LORD, nor fear the people of the land, for they are our bread; their protection has departed from them, and the LORD is with us. Do not fear them" (Num. 14:9, NKJV).

"They are our bread." What a bold statement! In other words, "They are not our problem; they are part of our provision!" I believe that once God had spoken to Joshua and Caleb, they rallied and said, "Hey, let's go possess this place. Let's go do it." In other words, "If God be for us, who can be against us?" (Rom. 8:31, KJV). "No giant can keep us out. These giants are bread for us— *lots* of bread!" That's how much Joshua and Caleb believed the Word of God.

Out of three million or more people who left Egypt's bondage, only two lived to see the Promised Land—not two million or two thousand, but *two*. Because of their belief in the Word of God and what He had instructed them to do, Joshua and Caleb possessed the land God had promised to His people. The rest of that generation died in the wilderness, even though the Promised Land was theirs for the taking.

GIANTS IN MY PROMISED LAND

The same principles hold true today. God promises us many things, but until we *possess* them, the promise remains *out there* somewhere, seemingly out of reach. You have to believe the Word and apply it. You have to know that God is on your side. If you fall, you need to know that you have an advocate in Jesus.

You and I have unique destinies that are bigger than we can imagine. The things He prepares for us are so mighty and incredible that we often need a shift in mind-set before we can accept them at face value. Until we make that shift in our hearts, the giants get the better of us. I know this is true because I have stood on the threshold of my promised land and questioned why I was there. Many a night standing on the stage, I have wondered, "What am I doing here? God, why have You chosen me? Why is my voice the one You want these people to hear tonight? What do I have to offer them?"

Then He reminds me that my calling was His idea. He reminds me that the giants intimidating God's people are not across the border in the promised land, but inside of us. They are insecurity giants and low-self-esteem giants and financial giants and I'm-not-ready giants. They are opportunists. They leap into action when God's promise is sleeping somewhere in the back of our minds. They hinder us when we forget that the Holy Spirit *always* gives us the words to speak and wisdom to follow. They exploit our doubts. When we forget, even for a moment, that God is for us and no one can be against us (as Romans 8:31 promises), we risk losing our promised land.

It is important to remember that whatever we face, we don't face it alone. God is in every moment with us. Once we know and accept this truth, our role in *taking the land* becomes simple: surrender to His plan and believe His Word.

It is amazing what happens when we *believe* that we can possess what He has promised!

LOVE, HOSPITALITY, AND THE PROMISE

One night while I was getting ready to preach, God revealed an entire sermon to me in just five minutes' time. Many days, whether I am preparing to preach or just doing my personal Bible study, I dig really deep into the Word. I had never had God speak to me the way He did on this night. In a handful of minutes, He downloaded a revelation from Scripture that He wanted me to preach that very night!

The passage He revealed was from 2 Kings 4. It is the story of Elisha and the Shunammite woman. Their relationship began when Elisha passed through Shunem and the woman invited him over for dinner. From that point on, she was hospitable to Elisha whenever he came to town. She knew he was a man of God with an anointing on his life. She valued the anointing and told her husband as much, saying, "Let's make a small room on the roof and put in it a bed and a table, a chair and a lamp for him. Then he can stay there whenever he comes to us" (2 Kings 4:10).

They built a room atop their house for Elisha. This act of love and hospitality pleased the prophet so much that he began to look for a way to bless them.

> One day when Elisha came, he went up to his room and lay down there. He said to his servant Gehazi, "Call the Shunammite." So he called her, and she stood before him. Elisha said to him, "Tell her, 'You have gone to all this trouble for us. Now what can be done for you? Can we speak on your behalf to the king or the commander of the army?'"
>
> —2 KINGS 4:11–13

The woman asked nothing of Elisha, but he persisted in his quest to bless her. His next question would change her life:

> "What can be done for her?" Elisha asked. Gehazi said, "Well, she has no son and her husband is old." Then Elisha said, "Call her." So he called her, and she stood in the doorway. "About this time next year," Elisha said, "you will hold a son in your arms." "No, my LORD," she objected. "Don't mislead your servant, O man of God!" But the woman became pregnant, and the next

year about that same time she gave birth to a son, just as Elisha had told her.

—2 KINGS 4:14–17

When Elisha first asked the Shunammite what she needed, she said, in essence, "I am content right here with my people. I am satisfied with where I am. It's all good." (See 2 Kings 4:13.) Yet, Gehazi perceived the desire of her heart. She longed for something her wealth could not provide: a son.

In ancient times, childbearing was in many ways seen as the measure of a woman. We know that the Shunammite was married to an aging man. It is likely that she was also up in years. As a childless wife, she had probably prayed for a child. The passage suggests that her dreams of motherhood were fading; we read that she was skeptical of Elisha's prophecy. In fact, she dared not believe it at first.

Like so many of us, she thought her prayers would never be answered. She was frank with the prophet and said, "Don't lie to me; don't make a promise that is going to mess with my emotions." Yet God had fulfillment in mind. He made good on the promise and gave her a son.

SHUTTING THE DOOR ON DOUBT

The fulfillment of a dream is never the end of the story. Even if you have waited all your life, the arrival of your dream is a beginning. Once the treasure is in your hand, you still have to believe God to keep it. Challenges will come; *giants* will try to steal what you have received from God. The Shunammite woman and her husband learned this the hard way.

The child grew, and one day he went out to his father, who was with the reapers. "My head! My head!" he said to his father. His father told a servant, "Carry him to his mother." After the servant had lifted him up and carried him to his mother, the boy sat on her lap until noon, and then he died.

—2 Kings 4:18–20

Imagine the emotional roller coaster this woman endured. First, she was promised a son, and the promise came to life. Now the promise was lying in her arms, dead. How alone she must have felt! Nonetheless, in her moment of despair, she put her faith in gear and found the strength to take a stand.

What she did next changed everything: "She went up and laid him on the bed of the man of God, then shut the door and went out" (2 Kings 4:21).

This woman understood the big picture. She remembered the way her promise had been delivered. Because it was a promise from God, she knew it was not destined for premature death. Instead of panicking, she brought her son's lifeless body to the place where his birth had been prophesied. Fighting the grief that surely tried to flood her soul, she literally closed the door on doubt, fear, and death.

Given her situation, it would have been easy to surrender and accept her son's death as the final word. No one would have been surprised if she camped out in that room and poured out her heart in tears. She might easily have said, "This is the worst thing that can happen to a mother, but it is what it is. I have to accept it and be content that this is it for my son and for me."

Wracked by loss, in a state of shock, it would seem perfectly natural to believe there was no other choice. Yet the Shunammite woman was convinced of the promise. It made her bold and unwilling to settle. She would not allow her son, who had come by way of a miracle, to be stolen. She called her husband and said, "Please send me one of the servants and a donkey so I can go to the man of God quickly and return" (2 Kings 4:22).

I like what she did; she was decisive. She shut the door behind her and said, "This thing is not over yet. I'm going to get the one who promised me this child and bring him back here with me."

That is exactly what she did. She went to Elisha, fell at his feet, and reminded him of the day he promised her a son. He saw her distress and instructed Gehazi to go with her and minister to the dead child.

Undeterred, the woman said, "As surely as the LORD lives and as you live, I will not leave you" (2 Kings 4:30). She knew it was Elisha and not Gehazi who had prophesied her son's birth. She knew the anointing of God was on Elisha, and she refused to leave without him.

As the Lord opened this passage to me in those minutes before service, He reminded me of Elijah's question to Elisha before the former was taken up to heaven: "Tell me, what can I do for you before I am taken from you?" (2 Kings 2:9).

Elisha was quick to respond: "Let me inherit a double portion of your spirit" (2 Kings 2:9). That double portion of the anointing was what brought the child to life a second time. The first portion was involved in his conception and birth.

The Bible tells what Elisha did when he returned to the room where the dead boy had been laid.

When Elisha reached the house, there was the boy lying dead on his couch. He went in, shut the door on the two of them and prayed to the LORD. Then he got on the bed and lay upon the boy, mouth to mouth, eyes to eyes, hands to hands. As he stretched himself out upon him, the boy's body grew warm. Elisha turned away and walked back and forth in the room and then got on the bed and stretched out upon him once more. The boy sneezed seven times and opened his eyes.

—2 KINGS 4:32–35

The first time Elisha lay on top of the boy, the child's body "grew warm" (the King James Version says he "waxed warm.") It was a resurrection, plain and simple—but it occurred in two stages. I believe restoration works the same way in our own lives; first we "wax warm," and then we let go of whatever was draining the life out of us.

A REPRESENTATIVE OF THE CHURCH

God drew me a parallel between the Shunammite's son and the body of Christ. When the boy cried out, "My head! My head!" I believe it was because he experienced pain. Whatever caused the pain is what took his life. It may be that he caught an ailment while he was out in the fields.

Our lives today are not lived entirely within the four walls of the church. We conduct much of our activity out in *the fields*, where we are exposed to philosophies, lifestyles, and other worldly influences. Like the Shunammite's son, we contract ailments that overtake us and cause our spirits to wither.

When we come to church, the atmosphere changes, at least for an hour or two. We are touched by the worship or the preaching of the Word. We sense God's power, and our hope is reignited. In other words, we wax warm. As the service closes, we know that we have been revived, yet over the course of the day or the week, we slip back into the frame of mind we were in before service started. We wonder why God's touch didn't last.

The answer is revealed in the second stage of the Shunammite boy's resurrection. After the first time, the boy's body grew warm. Yet Elisha was not satisfied; he lay on top of the boy again. After that, the boy sneezed seven times and opened his eyes.

The Bible does not present unnecessary details. There is a reason why the Scripture mentions seven sneezes. Both the act and the number of repetitions are meaningful. The boy's sneezing expelled something from his body. It may have been an irritant or toxic substance. Whatever it was, it needed to come out completely.

To the Hebrews, the number seven symbolized "perfection, fullness, abundance, rest, and completion."[1] It took seven sneezes—not two or four or five—to get the job done. Not only was the boy revived, as the warming of his body indicates, but he was also cleansed from all traces of whatever killed him. At that point, he opened his eyes. He became conscious of his life once again and was able to see that God had something more in store for him.

We are like that boy: we need to be refreshed, restored, even resurrected at times. But we need more than that. We need to get the junk out of our lives so that we can be transformed. Whether our junk is stored as anger or bitterness or the fear of failing again, we need to let it go. Whatever hurts have caused us to feel alone or frightened of the future—whether it is rejection, abandonment, betrayal, or disappointment—we need to leave it at the altar. If we hold on to it, it will destroy us.

This is what I believe God would say to the church: we need to find out what has been killing us out in the field. What is it that has been destroying our souls? What has been causing the spirit within each of us to wither? Is it negative talk? People on the job bringing us down? Distractions from what is important to God? Whatever it is, we must recognize it and let the sneezing begin.

The story of Elisha and the Shunammite's son also says something about how the anointing of God falls on a house. It may begin with the minister or the song leaders. Maybe a psalmist ushers in the presence of the Lord, and we camp there for a while. All of this is wonderful, yet we need to push beyond that place in Him— beyond the place of just "waxing warm." God wants to complete the transformation by getting us to "sneeze" until what is hurting us is expelled, and we are resurrected to a spiritual place we have not yet known.

He has already made the way for us. He laid all the necessary groundwork for us to possess the promises He has made. This is our time to believe His voice and shut the door on doubt.

We are not alone. God is on our side.

CHAPTER 4

FINDING HIS STRENGTH IN MY WEAKNESS

As I look at all the victories,
the Spirit rises up in me

And it's through the fire my
weakness is made strong!

SEEING STRENGTH IN OTHERS

DISPLAYS OF STRENGTH get our attention. We admire people whose inner discipline hoists them to the top of the ladder. We respect those whose wisdom reveals something solid within. We rely on those whose education or expertise can reinforce our efforts. Often we draw the greatest strength from those whose ordinary lives model extraordinary resilience.

The examples of others show us that we can be strong too. They raise our hopes and raise the bar. When we get down on ourselves, they remind us that a change for the better is possible. Most of all, their moments of weakness and struggle help us to remember that setbacks are part of being human. When we see others burst through barriers, we are inspired to demolish our own.

Sports provide great metaphors for life. For athletes, the competition is fierce, and winning means beating the odds. Who doesn't marvel at athletes who can do that? We root for the NBA star who is only six feet tall, the skier who races after a wipeout, the veteran slugger who aims for the fences year after year, the ghetto kid who found a path out of poverty and into the Hall of Fame.

Most fans sitting in the bleachers or reading the sports pages can tell you something about what makes these winners tick. In the days when my brothers and I lived and breathed basketball, we studied our Kentucky Wildcat heroes. We scoured their stats and even their life stories. We watched them, discussed them, and pinpointed each player's secret to success. We wanted to be just like them.

We could talk amongst ourselves about what worked on the court and what didn't. Yet those top-tier players were the only ones who could exemplify it for us. While we *talked* college basketball, they *lived* it. They were the ones who trained, learned the playbook, practiced shots, played hurt, faced contenders, and got up every morning and did it again.

The same is true spiritually. It is easy to talk about living for the Lord. We can recite the "thou shalts" and "thou shalt nots." We can name people who have served God. We admire and emulate them. We long to be like them, and with good reason—observing the lives of others is part of the process of spiritual growth. We learn from those whose examples speak for themselves.

A True Servant

As a family, the Crabb clan has had the benefit of strong examples. My parents and siblings have shown me the way more times than I can count, often without saying a word. From childhood, we learned to serve God. What our parents instilled in us has kept us, even when temptations to waver threatened.

Our parents weren't hatched from eggs, of course. Their parents passed on to them a spiritual heritage that has strengthened all of us and shaped our lives more than we know. My siblings and I have great parents *and* grandparents who prayed for us, taught us right from wrong, and imparted truth through the way they lived.

It would take a book to do justice to my family's heritage; a chapter for each of my grandparents would be just the start. For now, I will share one of the most important things my grandparents gave us: an example of how to serve God and love people. My mother's dad is a prime example. Granddad's testimony is powerful because he didn't just talk the talk—he truly walked the walk. Even if he had never said a word about how to live right, we would have learned it from Granddad. His daily life told us all we needed to know.

Granddad was a simple man. In his early years, he worked as a coal miner in Kentucky. When the mine closed, he bought a farm in Beaver Dam, Kentucky, the town where I grew up. He worked that farm and worked it hard. Granddad never shied away from work. He did whatever had to be done to care for his family and steward the land. As a youth, I spent many summers with him. We shared lots of time together, both in the fields and at the house when work was done.

The time we spent together was precious. Granddad had a tremendous impact on my life. He was not only a true servant of God, but he was also a servant to everyone he knew. Granddad was the type of man other people looked to for help. When something was broken or someone needed a hand, Granddad was the first one to show up. Even when his own equipment needed fixing, Granddad would help the neighbors first. It is the way he operated all the time. Everyone who knew him would tell you this: you could rely on Granddad to help gather the crops or meet a need any time of the day or night.

My granddad was a kind man. When he had a moment to sit on the porch of his and Grandma's house, he always had a friendly wave for passersby. He was the kind of man Paul the apostle described as living a life worthy of the Lord and pleasing to Him in every way. (See Colossians 1:10.)

Not only that, but Granddad was one of the best tractor men in Kentucky.

Whoever serves me must follow me; and where I am, my servant also will be. My Father will honor the one who serves me.

—JOHN 12:26

STRENGTH IN PRAYER

One of my favorite stories about Granddad involves his partner—his old John Deere tractor. He had it so long that the seat eventually rusted out. That didn't stop Granddad. He was resourceful and could fix just about anything. When the seat gave way, he took one of Grandma's kitchen chairs, sawed off the legs, and fastened the seat onto his tractor. When he plowed the fields, Granddad looked like he was seated at the dinner table!

What a special guy he was! Granddad enjoyed his work and loved the outdoors. He loved rolling up his sleeves and producing a crop. Come what may, you could find Granddad in the fields, working. He had a passion for working under the sun (or the moon) for as many hours as it took to get the job done. The only thing Granddad loved more than farming was getting me in the fields to farm with him.

My granddad was a strong, vibrant man, physically and otherwise. Yet there came a time when his physical strength began to fail. He eventually went for a checkup and was diagnosed with throat cancer. Nobody but Granddad knows how big a blow that was. Yet neither he nor my grandmother was diminished by it. Granddad worked as long and hard as he could, and Grandma went to the mat and wrestled in prayer for her man. She was an anointed woman who could pray a camel through the eye of a needle. Her prayers for Granddad were answered too: he beat cancer twice!

In 2007, however, the cancer returned. Still, my granddad refused to quit. The day after his throat surgery, he put on a mask, got in his combine, and harvested his bean crop. He was determined to get that crop in. It took him all night to do it. Although Granddad remained strong in spirit, his body grew weaker over time. There came a day when he could no longer farm. I watched his life change dramatically; we all did. One thing led to another, and soon Granddad had to let the yard work go. After a while, he lost the ability to walk outside. Even waving to passersby became an effort.

Seeing Granddad in that state broke my heart. I knew it was hard for him to accept physical limitations. The inability to work and enjoy the outdoors was crushing to a man like him. As unimaginable as it was, there came a time when Granddad became bedridden and was unable to do any of the things he loved doing.

It was tough for everyone—*really* tough. Yet even in Granddad's time of physical weakness, he was a picture of strength. It was the kind of strength that comes not from what you can do but from who you are. That is inspiring; it is the strength shown by those who live *in Christ*.

THE FISHING TRIP

Jesus never papered over the reality of human weakness. Instead, He helped His disciples to recognize their frailties as part of their humanity. The night before He was crucified (and before Peter denied Him), Jesus encouraged Peter to pray and become aware of temptation, warning the disciple that "the spirit indeed is willing, but the flesh is weak" (Matt. 26:41, KJV)

Jesus came *because* we are prone to weakness and sin. By nature the flesh yields to the very things that pull us away from God. Have you ever heard anyone design a plan for failure? Has anyone ever said to you, "Today I am going to stray from God. I'm fixin' to backslide and break my Savior's heart"? I've seen people backslide, but I've never heard anyone announce it in advance!

Backsliding is not something you choose from a menu. It is something you fall into gradually, often without realizing it. My dad wrote a song about sin and backsliding; it's called "The Shepherd's Call." The song talks about God's love and redemption, but it also explains how we drift from God:

> I wandered far from the fold where I was safe.
> It wasn't long until I found I'd lost my way.[1]

When I was just a boy, God gave me an object lesson about the subject. He did it through what promised to be an exciting adventure: a fishing trip. Fishing stories and fisherman seem to figure big in Scripture. Jesus chose several fishermen to be on His team, and He often taught them through experiences on the water. (See John 21:1–6; Matthew 13:47–50.) In fact, when He called Peter (then known as Simon) and Andrew, He made an analogy using fishing:

> As Jesus walked beside the Sea of Galilee, he saw Simon and
> his brother Andrew casting a net into the lake, for they were

fishermen. "Come, follow me," Jesus said, "and I will make you fishers of men." At once they left their nets and followed him.

—MARK 1:16–18

It is not surprising that a fishing experience became a life lesson for me. It was my first time fishing in a boat on the river. I was ecstatic to be there and eager to haul in some catfish. For a kid from Beaver Dam, this was a dream come true!

Three of us set out that day: a buddy of mine, his father, and me. We started early that morning as the fog rose on the river. As we cruised downstream, my friend's dad said, "This looks like the spot. Son, grab that anchor and throw it over." Before he could drop the anchor, we already had our lines in the water. We couldn't wait to get started. We loved fishing and hunting like almost nothing else.

Right at the outset, I thought I had a bite. In reality, my line was tangled. I grabbed the pole and tried to set the hook. Everyone reached for their poles at the same time, and—you guessed it—my line got tangled up in theirs.

Suddenly my friend's dad looked around and asked, "What happened? This is not where we anchored down. Son, did you throw in that anchor like I told you to?"

"Yes, Dad," he answered.

We soon discovered that although the anchor was attached to a rope, the rope was not tied to the boat. The anchor was lodged in the riverbed, but we had drifted downstream of it. Without realizing it, we had been adrift the whole time, far from where we started out.

That is exactly what happens when we backslide. Spiritually speaking, we end up someplace unexpected, unaware that we have been traveling in the wrong direction for some time. Often the downstream journey starts when we forget that weakness is part of being human, and strength—*genuine* strength—is found only when we are anchored in Christ.

ANCHORED IN CHRIST

The writer of Hebrews describes the benefits of being anchored in Christ. We read that God's purpose is unchangeable and trustworthy in its very nature. (See Hebrews 6:17.) The writer of Hebrews goes on to say, "We have this hope as an anchor for the soul, firm and secure" (Heb. 6:19). Anchored to Christ, we are always on solid ground.

One night I was on stage singing "The Shepherd's Call" when that memorable fishing trip came to mind. So many things about it were significant. I thought about how calm the river looked on the surface and how strong the current was underneath. I thought about how easily we can be deceived in life. Often we *drown* in smooth waters because we don't recognize the strength of the undercurrents. Sometimes we overestimate the seaworthiness of our vessel and ignore the weather and the tides. At other times we fail to rig our equipment properly, as my friend, his father, and I had done with our anchor all those years ago.

Even when the waters of life are as smooth as glass, you can find yourself off course. It can happen at any time. Undercurrents can take you by surprise even when your spiritual life seems to be cruising right along. It is an age-old trick of the enemy to try to gain the upper hand in increments. He is patient and subtle. He draws us away with distractions too miniscule to set off our internal alarms. Before we realize we are in trouble, we have swallowed the deception—hook, line, and sinker.

I have been there, and I can tell you, it does not happen overnight. Little by little my focus got off. I got caught up in the business of ministry and music. The Crabb Family was on the road, clicking on all cylinders. It was, in a way, intoxicating, as though nothing could go wrong. I remember one night walking onto the stage for sound check. The concert was sold out, the music was flowing, the acoustics fell into place. I thought, "Man, this is going to be great!"

God got a hold of me in a hurry. He said, "You are leaving out something—Me." His words hit me hard, right in the gut. For the first three songs, I was miserable. The correction God gave me was dead on. I had put down anchor, but my rope wasn't attached to Him. That night, with just a few words, He shook everything in me that could be shaken and brought me back to basics: my gifts for singing and making music were not about me or how good I was; it all came from Him and from how good He is.

I learned just how easily our gifts can become our curse. The devil will use anything he can to draw us away from God. He is a master of the sneak approach; it's one of his favorite and most effective tactics. He lulls us into admiring the smooth surface of the waters, while the raging current underneath is ready to swallow us up and hold us under.

The only real security we have is in our Anchor. When we are attached to Him, He keeps us from drifting downstream. He keeps us from entanglements on the river, on stage, at home, or wherever He leads us. He keeps our weaknesses from overtaking us, and He brings *His* strength into play on our behalf.

Cut the Line and Start Over

Here's another fishing tip: sometimes, when your line gets tangled, the best thing you can do is cut it and start over!

Cutting the line doesn't mean you can't bring in a catch. It just means that fishing trips don't always go as planned. Sometimes you come home with more fish than you can give away, and sometimes your fishing trip ends up being a sightseeing cruise. It's not the end of the world; you still have plenty of line to work with and other opportunities for a catch. You can cut the line that got you into trouble and start over.

When things go wrong, our default is often to try and force them right. We want to preserve our intent and untangle the line. Yet often there isn't time to undo the mess. It isn't always possible to reverse the damage we have done. That is when you do the only thing that makes sense: you cut the line, cut your losses, and start again. You take a new hook and go fishing!

This is as true in our everyday affairs as it is in fishing. It is also true in ministry—for preachers, gospel singers, and the individual soul winner. There are too many fish to catch for you to quit now. The tangle you were in does not disqualify you from being a fisher of lost souls. You may have to cut a whole lot of line, but there is more where that came from. And your new hook is sharp; it may be a better hook than you have ever had in your tackle box: it is the testimony you can share about how God freed you from the tangle of sin!

When you come through the fire—any fire—you come out the other side with tools you never had before. Those tools (wisdom, understanding, your testimony, a deeper knowledge of God) are not forged when the river is cooperating and the wind is at your back. They are forged when you are under pressure and feeling the heat. You may get a little banged up, but you learn the things no one and no situation can take from you.

I shared earlier how thankful I am to be married to Shellye. We have a wonderful marriage and the best kids in the world. So much of that is true because of the kind of person Shellye is and the kind of relationship we have as a result. I love her so deeply I can't put it into words. Yet like most mates, I miss the mark at times—maybe more times than I know. There was a particular time after we had been married awhile that this happened; it was a time when I got caught up in life and, without realizing it, took Shellye for granted.

Living like that will put a chill into the best of relationships. I felt it. We *both* felt it. We were at that place where you have to cut the line and start fresh, or the fishing trip is over. I'm not talking about severing the marriage; the line we needed to cut involved the sin that had crept into my attitude and affected our relationship. It was weighing us down and pulling us downstream.

I can remember the conversation we had when these issues finally surfaced. We were at the point where something had to be done. We were both in tears; it was painful. Yet even our pain bore fruit, because it got us focused on what mattered. To this day, I thank God for waking us up to the situation.

We didn't necessarily understand everything that had happened. It was not as though there had been a traumatic event or an argument that drove a wedge between us. It was more subtle than that. I had developed the habit of living day to day without letting Shellye know how important she was to me. Little by little, we drifted apart.

There was a lot we didn't know, but one thing was clear: we loved each other enough to lay our cards on the table. We knew we had to get back to what made us the couple we had always been. We cut away the tangled-up line and fell in love all over again. Day by day, our love grew stronger and more grounded. Our wake-up call gave us another chance, for which I am eternally grateful.

If the devil's sneak attack has caught you off guard, turn the tables on him. Take what he meant for harm and use it for good. People can draw strength from your testimony and even find a way out of their own messes because of it. Suddenly your story of cutting the line can free up someone else and even be used by God to lead that person to Christ. As the apostle John wrote, "Anyone who believes in the Son of God has this testimony in his heart" (1 John 5:10). Because of God's love and power, your testimony can be a lifeline to someone else.

All is not lost when you start over. Even when you cut your line, what really matters is still with you: you still have your Anchor, who is Christ; and you have a good, strong rope, which is His Word! No hidden current or raging storm can compete with that kind of strength!

Ray Boltz said it perfectly in his song "The Anchor Holds":

Though the ship is battered
The anchor holds
Though the sails are torn...
The anchor holds.[2]

"I'M AMAZED"

One of the most rewarding experiences my family and I ever had was to sing at the Brooklyn Tabernacle and visit with Pastor Jim Cymbala and his dear wife, Sister Carol, who leads the choir. Theirs is among the most amazing ministries I have witnessed in my entire life.

The Brooklyn Tabernacle is a church like no other. It is a place where worshipers praise God not out of habit or duty or religion but out of genuine relationship with their Creator. The worship is so pure. It is not self-conscious or showy, yet it is moving beyond description. I've watched Pastor Cymbala sitting on the side of the platform, his eyes closed and hands raised, with tears streaming down his cheeks as he worships the King. He is the epitome of humility before God and man, a man willing to be *weak* so that the strength of Christ shines through.

In reality, Pastor Cymbala is strong—in faith, in dedication to the gospel, and in love. So is Sister Carol. She has a tremendous heart for worship and for people, especially those who are forgotten, whether on the streets or in prison. The Cymbalas are an inspiration to everyone who meets them.

Some years ago the Crabb Family did a live video at the Brooklyn Tabernacle. Making that video was tremendous fun, although I was nervous about it at first. It was especially rewarding to sing with the Brooklyn Tabernacle Choir. There is just something about having all those voices harmonizing behind you. It is powerful.

Some time after making the live video at the Brooklyn Tabernacle, I received a call from Bryan Hudson that rocked my world. Bryan is a dear friend and the manager of the beloved gospel group the

Martins. He has a deep love for ministry and has been a great blessing to my family and me. I cannot thank him enough for some of the doors he has been instrumental in opening in my life. Bryan called that day and said, "Sister Carol wants to know if you'd be interested in singing a song on the new Brooklyn Tabernacle record."

I'll never forget the thoughts that raced through my mind: "I can't believe this! This is amazing! Say what?"

Before beginning the recording, the Cymbalas invited me to visit with them at a studio in Nashville. They wanted me to listen to a song they were writing and let them know what I thought about it. (You can imagine my amazement at such a request!) I met with Larry Goss and Sister Carol, and together we listened to the song. The lyrics had not yet been completed, but I was pretty sure God was up to something with the music. Larry Goss seemed excited about the song and even about my being involved. Nobody was more excited than I was. I heard the music and said, "You can count me in. I'll be there. It's an honor."

The process of putting this live production together was unusual. Typically you record the song in the studio and then make a live video set to the music you have already recorded. In this case, the live video was going to be made first. It was a challenge for me. I didn't know why at the time, but I had the hardest time learning the lyrics. I sang the song countless times. I even slept with my iPod so the lyrics could roll around in my head all night. I sang that song every chance I got, including during sound checks with Justin, my keyboardist at the time. I not only sang the song, but I also wrote out the lyrics to help me memorize them.

When the day came to do the live video at Brooklyn Tabernacle, my family was in the midst of a crazy time. Issues and schedules were colliding, and I had gotten no more than thirty minutes of sleep in a forty-eight-hour period. I was exhausted and scheduled to sing on stage with the Brooklyn Tabernacle's famous choir for the live taping of a song I had struggled to learn!

My mind was anything but focused on the task at hand. If ever I had felt weak or unable to rise to the occasion, this was it. The thought of how badly I could mess things up drove me to distraction. I came dangerously close to calling the Cymbalas and telling them I couldn't come. The situation was so out of control, I knew I was under an all-out attack of the enemy. Somehow I made my flight. When taping started around midday on Sunday, I was there.

The battle was far from over. Once on stage, I experienced the most profound sense of panic I had ever known. The issue I had been dealing with since hearing this song escalated: the music began, and the lyrics escaped my mind. Even the opening line of the song was erased from my memory.

It was a mess; *I* was a mess. The church pews were full of people who had come to be part of the event. Everyone was pumped up and in position, from musicians to crew to the Cymbalas. The 260-member choir was waiting. The cameras were ready to roll. My mind was a complete blank.

Finally, I said to the congregation, "I'll just be honest with you. I don't think I have ever had to fight so hard to learn lyrics as I have for this song. But it lets me know one thing for sure: when we get through this; it's going to minister to a lot of people."

To get through the videotaping, I scooted close to Sister Carol. Sweet woman that she is, she mouthed the lyrics for me as I sang. Finally, after I stopped the taping three times, we nailed the song. I thank God for it. "I'm Amazed" is the title cut of the album...and God had big plans for it.

Look at the nations and watch—and be utterly amazed. For I am going to do something in your days that you would not believe, even if you were told.
—HABAKKUK 1:5

A DREAM COME TRUE

A short time later, I received a call to go to Angola, Louisiana, to sing at the Louisiana State Penitentiary with the Brooklyn Tabernacle Choir. Sister Carol wanted me to sing the song "I'm Amazed" for the prisoners. It was an outstanding event. Sister Carol and I sang with the choir. Pastor Cymbala gave an altar call and ministered salvation to the inmates.

One of the inmates was so touched by the event that he called the Cymbalas when he was about to be released from prison. He had no one to come get him or to help him get on his feet, but they met the need. Amazingly, he relocated to Brooklyn and became part of their church family.

I was still traveling with the Crabb Family at the time. Our road schedule was intense, so we rarely took vacations. When we did get breaks, we made the most of them and spent the time with our families. Six to eight months after recording "I'm Amazed," Sister Carol got on the phone and said, "Hey, I'd really like for you to come to New York. I know you're on vacation, but I just wanted to ask you if you'd sing, 'I'm Amazed' at an event we are doing."

I hesitated and said, "Well, maybe I can make it work."

She told me the date of the event, and I said, "That's right in the middle of our vacation." Then I asked, "What kind of event is it?"

She said, "Billy Graham is doing his last crusade here in New York, and I wondered if you'd sing the song with us."

I started to say, "Let me think about it," and then blurted out, "Yes. I'll be there."

The crusade lasted three days, from June 24 through June 26, 2005. More than two hundred thousand people attended. There were seventy thousand chairs and three overflow areas arranged on ninety-three acres at Flushing Meadows Park. JumboTrons helped the massive crowd to see what was happening on the platform, and the famous Unisphere from the 1964–1965 World's Fair stood 140 feet tall behind the crusade grounds.[3]

What an event it was! Each day Billy Graham walked across the platform slowly, looking like a modern-day Moses with silvery white hair. He preached daily, and thousands accepted Christ after each message (a total of more than eight thousand souls over three days).[4]

It was an event of great spiritual consequence, and for whatever reason, God ordained "I'm Amazed" to be part of the service that Sunday. I believe that is the reason the enemy fought the song so hard in the beginning. Today I get lots of requests for the song, and I love singing it, even without the five-hundred-voice choir that sang at the crusade!

More than the song, I dearly love Pastor Cymbala and Sister Carol. They are true servants of God. Even the weekend of the

Billy Graham Crusade, with all that was going on, Pastor Cymbala held service at the Brooklyn Tabernacle. Other men might have suspended church that week, but Pastor Cymbala said, "What if someone comes needing to hear a message of hope? It might be just one, but we have to have service in case that one shows up."

They are two of the most precious people I have ever met. I will never forget God's strength working divinely through them. I will forever be grateful to them for wrapping me in their arms of love and giving me the kinds of opportunities most people only dream of.

Even when weakness tries to overtake the plan of God, His plans and His favor prevail.

> *The LORD is near to all who call on him, to all who call on him in truth. He fulfills the desires of those who fear him...*
>
> —PSALM 145:18–1

THE HEALING POWER OF GOD

There are so many memorable services I have been privileged to witness. One night we ministered at a church where God moved in a mighty way. You could feel His presence in the house. People came to the altar and got saved. Some rededicated their lives to Him. Tremendous things happened that night. People's hearts were changed, and bodies were healed.

During the service I called out a man from the congregation. This is something I rarely do. It makes me nervous to step out that way; you really have to know that you know that it is God before you can do so. But when He lays something heavy on my heart the way He did that night, I do what He says.

I told the man, "I want to pray for you. God wants to do something in your life. He wants to touch you and heal you." I did not know that the man couldn't raise his left arm. He had pulled all the ligaments and tendons, and his range of motion was extremely limited.

I said, "Sir, raise your hands toward heaven and begin to praise the Lord as we pray."

He raised the only arm he could raise, his right arm. He must have been thinking, "Oh, God, please don't let Jason grab my left arm and raise it in the air. It hurts enough as it is."

Of course, not realizing the pain this man was enduring, I grabbed his arm and raised it straight up over his head! He began to cry, shout, and praise God. Then he began slinging his arm around wildly, praising God for the instantaneous healing he received in that service. People began coming to the altar. Perhaps they knew this man's medical history; I really don't know. I do know they received Christ as their Savior and were set free from all kinds of situations. The people laid their *stuff* down at the altar that night and left it there.

Between being nervous about calling out this man and then risking serious injury to his already damaged arm, my weaknesses were out there for everyone to see. Yet God, in His great mercy, grace, and power, saw to it that His will was done. It was a powerful, powerful night.

> *By faith in the name of Jesus, this man whom you*
> *see and know was made strong. It is Jesus' name and*
> *the faith that comes through him that has given this*
> *complete healing to him, as you can all see.*
>
> —ACTS 3:16

"PLEASE FORGIVE ME"

One night at a concert in Alabama we sang "Please Forgive Me." At the time, it was a new song that my dad had written. We were just about ready to release the song to radio stations, but it had not yet gotten any airplay.

This particular concert was held in a Baptist church that seated just two hundred fifty people, although I'm sure there were three hundred fifty people in attendance. It was a great night. There were folks packed in from wall to wall with chairs wedged everywhere, even out in the hall. There were even some people outside the church who watched the concert through the windows.

Before we sang Dad's new song that night, we knew it was anointed. Even so, we did not realize how powerfully the people would respond to it. Almost from the start of the first verse, people got up from their seats. Some came down front, including couples that came holding hands and praying together. Soon people were in the aisles praying. Whole families were praying!

It was one of the first times we had sung "Please Forgive Me," and I'm sure we sang it through at least sixteen times that night. It was a supernatural service. The convicting power of the Lord fell, and He drew people to Himself. Thirty-eight people gave their hearts to

Him in that church. The song with one of the most humbling titles imaginable was used by God that night, and mightily.

"Who can forgive sins but God alone?"
—LUKE 5:21

By the end of the service, I could barely talk, partly because there was nothing else to say and partly because we had sung so long. The main thing was that the glory of God had fallen on that place. It was strong. Some couples testified that before the service their marriages were about to disintegrate. They came so close to splitting up, but right there, God healed their marriages!

That night in Alabama our ministry started taking off in a big way. Today that concert remains one of my most precious memories. Some of the people who attended service that night still come to our concerts. There is a connection between them and us; it is a strong connection that only God could forge.

THE ALTAR CALL SONG

When disc jockeys across America started playing Dad's song "Please Forgive Me," it became the highest-charted song on the radio stations that reported airplay. In fact, it charted higher than any song ever had in Southern Gospel music. It stayed at number one for four or five months, which is a long time in that genre.

I wish I had kept a record of all the testimonies we received as a result of that song. Radio stations and listeners called "Please Forgive Me," the "altar-call song," because it generated so many testimonies. It was not unusual for folks to call radio stations and ask, "Would you please play the altar-call song?"

I shared in the Introduction about the day we learned that "Please Forgive Me" had hit number one. Our bus was grounded by a blowout when someone called our cell phone to say the song had topped the charts. It was an exciting moment, even though we were sitting just off the road stuck as we could be with a tire that was done for. The irony was stark: a broken-down bus and a number-one song. I guess it was a good thing; had we been driving down the highway, we probably would have wrecked the bus on hearing that we had our first number-one hit!

ALWAYS FAITHFUL, ALWAYS STRONG

There has been lots of water under the bridge for my family and me: lots of trying times and steep hills to climb, both personally and as a ministry. All of it has made us the people we are today—people with rough edges still needing to be smoothed over and lessons still to be learned, but people whose faith has been strengthened and enlarged by His merciful hand.

Through thick and thin and all of the outstanding opportunities I have experienced over the years, God has been faithful. He has done unimaginable things in ways that are so creative and timely as to boggle my mind.

Still, there will always be those moments, hopefully fewer and farther between, in which I see my human weakness as a barrier to the miraculous. Even then—*especially* then—I know He will do as He has done my whole life long: He will reveal Himself in all His glory and weakness. Doubt will have no choice but to fade away.

My soul finds rest in God alone; my salvation comes from him. He alone is my rock and my salvation; he is my fortress, I will never be shaken.

—PSALM 62:1–2

CHAPTER 5

COUNTING THE COST
OF CHRISTIANITY

*He never promised that the
cross would not get heavy*

*And the hill would not
be hard to climb!*

CLAY ON DISPLAY

EVERYTHING GOD CREATES is a masterpiece. *We* are His masterpieces. When the works of His hands become damaged or worn, He restores them. When they cease to function as He intended, He makes whatever adjustments are needed.

God did not create us to desert us. In Christ, He paid an enormous price so that we could remain in fellowship with Him. God desires to be involved in our lives. He longs to guide us and, when necessary, to restore us. Like the potter who turns a drab clump of clay into something wonderful, God keeps us on His wheel. Day by day He perfects us, and when we become nicked or marred, He reworks the pieces of our brokenness until the vessel is more beautiful than when He first created it.

I don't know about you, but sometimes I feel more like *a piece of work* than a masterpiece. I felt that way during the recording of "I'm Amazed" at the Brooklyn Tabernacle. Imagine being invited to sing the title cut for an amazing album in the company of legends like Carol Cymbala and the Brooklyn Tabernacle Choir, only to forget the words! (See chapter 4.)

Yet God did not leave me in pieces on that stage or in that project. He carried me through and accomplished His desire through the song He had me sing. He also used the experience to mold me. He kept His potter's wheel turning and reshaped some of the clay; He smoothed out some of the lumps and made this vessel more useful to His service.

In the grand scheme of things, the taping of "I'm Amazed" was just a bump in the road. Yet there's no telling what blessings and ministry opportunities might have been missed had I walked off the platform without finishing my assignment that day. I believe that assignment was a heavenly one; it affects my life to this day.

Still, I have faced larger hurdles in my lifetime. There have been seasons during which I lost sight of things: the source of my gifts, the preciousness of my wife, the way forward. There was also a season where I lost sight of my identity in God. It was a time during which bitterness began to take root in me, and I wandered off God's path. It was a traumatic time that I intend to share a little later on in this book.

It is a wonder to me that the clay that is *me* did not disintegrate at any of these points along the way. Quite the opposite is true: whenever cracks appear in this vessel, the warm hands of my Father rework the clay and restore me so that I might serve others, fulfill my calling, and glorify Him.

Not all of life is pretty. Often our brokenness sticks out like a sore thumb. Even the restoration process can be messy. Life has a way of becoming complicated, even when we try hard to keep it simple. Yet I know there is something beautiful about all of it. Speaking for myself, the beautiful part is the fact that I have never been forsaken by God. Not only that, but He has also given me a platform to tell you that you aren't forsaken, either.

That is why I am happy to share my life in all its imperfection and say, "Here it is—no pretenses or illusions. Take from my story what you will. If it gives even one person hope enough to hold on, it will have been worth it."

If that is not what our lives are for, then I haven't got a clue why we are here. I believe it is about receiving God's grace and extending that grace to help somebody else. I can't do that and present a sanitized version of myself. I have got to keep it as real as I can, or grace will drop out of the equation. I cannot worry about whether I am striking the right pose or creating the right impression. I have to be willing to know and be known for who I really am.

That, I believe, is part of the price of authentic Christianity. If I forget, even for a moment, that I am as prone to making mistakes as the next guy, then I need to take another trip to the altar. And whether I realize my missteps or I don't, I can rest assured that I have a permanent invitation to the Potter's wheel.

Jesus paid His part of the price. By comparison, mine is a pittance.

Humble yourselves, therefore, under God's mighty
hand, that he may lift you up in due time

—1 PETER 5:6

THE MOLDING PROCESS

After years on the road, I am still astounded by the fact that God planted His dream in my heart. It's like I said in the Introduction: I never had to wonder or question why I was here. I was born to sing, and for years that was all I needed to know on the subject.

My earliest memory of fulfilling that dream goes back to when I was just two years old. God knows that I had not been walking long, yet I was ready to sing at the Church of Philadelphia in Horse Branch, Kentucky! My dad stood me up on the altar with my little acoustic guitar, and as he played his own guitar, I sang an old song entitled "Who Is the Lord Our God?"

As I look back at those days, I see how God was molding me and preparing me to do what I am doing now. It is hard to fathom the perfection involved in the plan of God. I remember singing as a child and experiencing His presence as I sang. Not only was He there, but He was also involved in my singing of the song. It goes to show just how receptive children are to the things of God!

The memory of His presence on that day is, for me, a reminder that I have been on His track all along, even before I could have fully understood it. I could not have predicted (and still can't predict) exactly where the path will take me or what the cost will be along the way.

Not even the patriarchs of the Bible knew all that God was calling them to do. Imagine what went on in Abram's mind when God said, "Leave your country, your people and your father's household and go to the land I will show you" (Gen. 12:1). God didn't say, "…the land I *have* shown you"; He said, "…the land I *will* show you."

God told Abram to pack up his family and head out to an undisclosed location. That's a tall order. It is one thing to move on; it is another to hit the road without a destination in mind. Yet that is what God asked, and He did it so Abram could achieve the fullness of his destiny.

Obeying God even when you do not understand is the essence of the walk of faith and an important element in the molding process. It is also enough to ruffle your feathers. God's request had to have pushed Abram to the outer limits of his understanding. Abram faced what Sue Monk Kidd calls a *crisis* in her book *When the Heart Waits*. The crisis she speaks of is not a random event; it is a divine appointment designed to lead us somewhere in particular.

A crisis of this kind is a "holy summons to cross a threshold. It involves both a leaving behind and a stepping forward, a separation and an opportunity."[1] When it is recognized, a holy summons strengthens your faith.

Still, doubt will enter in at times, even when you are sure about your calling. Knowing that I was created to sing did not insulate me from moments of hesitation or concern. Instead, it has molded me and helped me to process my doubts more accurately. That is why the memory from the Church of Philadelphia in Horse Branch is so valuable: it reminds me to keep going and never quit, regardless of the circumstances I face.

I have to take that stand every day. Every day I must refuse to let the devil put a lid on my dreams. I won't let him cheat me out of doing God's work. I will not relinquish the cup prepared for me by my Father in heaven. The price my Savior paid for that cup was too high for me to take it lightly.

Let This Cup Pass From Me

There is a passage from Scripture that never fails to capture my heart, because it describes the price of salvation as clearly as words can. In it we hear Jesus's words to the Father as the Son contended with the ultimate crisis.

> Jesus went out as usual to the Mount of Olives, and his disciples followed him. On reaching the place, he said to them, "Pray that you will not fall into temptation." He withdrew about a stone's throw beyond them, knelt down and prayed,

"Father, if you are willing, take this cup from me; yet not my
will, but yours be done."

—LUKE 22:39–42

When Jesus submitted Himself to the Father's will and all that it
entailed, He crossed a threshold; it was the place where crisis and
opportunity would collide. He knew He had been born for this
purpose, and He sold out to it completely. What a moment it must
have been in the heavens!

It is riveting to read about Jesus's prayers the night before He was
crucified. Seeing the place during a trip to Israel where it is believed
He prayed adds another dimension altogether. Of all the sights
and experiences in the Holy Land, the Garden of Gethsemane has
affected me perhaps more than any other.

And there are so many. Visiting Galilee stirred my imagina-
tion. So did sitting on the temple steps in Jerusalem where the
moneychangers' tables were overturned. Walking down the Via
Dolorosa is unforgettable too. It is hard to believe that your feet are
touching some of the very stone steps Jesus's own feet tread upon
two thousand years ago.

The Holy Land brings the facts of our faith to life. One building
sticks out in my mind above all others. It's called the Church of
All Nations. The name commemorates the many countries that
contributed to its construction. It is located on the Mount of Olives
in Jerusalem next to the Garden of Gethsemane, where Jesus spent
His final earthly night in prayer.

Inside the church, in front of the altar, is a large rock. It is
believed to be the stone upon which Jesus prayed on that fateful
night. The stone is surrounded by a crown-of-thorns fence made

of wrought iron. We were fortunate enough to go inside the fence, where people are rarely permitted to go. When we stepped inside, we sensed something really powerful about the place. Sorrow stirred in my spirit, as though I could feel the weight of the price Jesus paid. We laid our hands on that rock as we prayed and took Communion there. I will never forget the experience.

The Olive Trees

Something else about the place got hold of me: the olive trees. I remember hearing someone nearby our group saying, "These are some of the oldest olive trees in the world." Some of the trees are believed to be a couple of thousand years old!

To this day, I cannot get those trees out of my mind. As I stood in their midst, I thought about all that happened there the night before Jesus died. We know from the Scriptures that Jesus took His disciples to the Mount of Olives. He wanted them to pray, but every time He checked on them, He found them sleeping. He asked Peter, "Simon…are you asleep? Could you not keep watch for one hour?" (Mark 14:37).

Even on the most excruciating night of His earthly walk, Jesus loved His disciples and extended grace to them. He understood their human weaknesses. With so much at stake, He tried to keep them tracking with Him spiritually but eventually let it go. He as much as said, "Go ahead. Get some rest. Tomorrow is going to be the toughest day you have ever known."

Jesus returned to the stone and prayed the most consequential prayer of all time: "Yet not my will, but yours be done" (Luke 22:42). The history of humanity pivoted in that moment. There was no turning back. The heavens were in motion, and the events of the weekend would determine man's fate for all eternity.

Jesus's suffering had just begun. Already the pressure of His ordeal was so great that He began to sweat drops of blood, as Luke described: "And being in anguish, he prayed more earnestly, and his sweat was like drops of blood falling to the ground" (Luke 22:44). Imagine the intensity of the battle Jesus waged in prayer. He knew He was about to take on the sins of the world. It was a price so exorbitant that only He, the Father, and the Holy Spirit could have understood it.

This very consequential prayer would prove to be *the* prayer that gives all of us hope. It was the prayer that said, "It's all settled. The mission will soon be completed. I will not turn back. I accept this burden. With joy, I will do all it takes to bridge the gap that stands between a holy God and sin-laden humankind. I *will* pay the price." (See Hebrews 12:2.)

Luke 22:44 says that as Jesus prayed, the drops of His blood fell "to the ground." The blood of the Savior—the blood that redeems us—seeped into the earth surrounding those olive trees. I asked Perry Stone, a dear minister friend whom I love and respect, about the history of the olive trees. He told me that when the Romans took over the region, they tried to destroy everything in sight.

He then said, "Why do you ask about the trees?"

I shared with Perry the thoughts that were rolling around in my head. I had this mental picture of a man working the fields in the heat of the day. With every step, sweat dripped off his face and soaked the ground. I thought about when Jesus interrupted His Gethsemane prayer to check on His disciples. He had been sweating too. I pictured that sweat—the great drops of blood being forced through His pores—falling to the ground with every step He took. Those drops had fallen where the olive trees stand to this day. I told Perry, "No wonder they are some of the oldest trees in the world. Whatever His blood touches can't help but live!"

Perry said, "That makes the history of those trees even more amazing because, even if every one of them had been cut down by the Romans, the roots were still under the surface. That blood would have gotten to those roots and brought those trees back to life above the surface!"

Everything Jesus did cost Him. And everything He did blessed us.

It Is Finished

Recently I preached on the twentieth chapter of the Book of John. The chapter starts out with Mary Magdalene's discovery that Jesus's body was not in the tomb:

> Early on the first day of the week, while it was still dark, Mary Magdalene went to the tomb and saw that the stone had been removed from the entrance. So she came running to Simon Peter and the other disciple, the one Jesus loved, and said, "They have taken the Lord out of the tomb, and we don't know where they have put him!" So Peter and the other disciple started for the tomb. Both were running, but the other disciple outran Peter and reached the tomb first. He bent over and looked in at the strips of linen lying there but did not go in. Then Simon Peter, who was behind him, arrived and went into the tomb. He saw the strips of linen lying there, as well as

the burial cloth that had been around Jesus' head. The cloth was folded up by itself, separate from the linen.

—JOHN 20:1–7

The last two verses in this passage explain that the disciples saw the presumably rumpled linen strips (that had been wrapped around Jesus's body) and the folded napkin (that had covered His head) lying on the floor of the tomb in separate places. John made it a point to describe the different conditions and locations of the two kinds of cloth. Since he wrote under the influence of the Holy Spirit, I have to believe that the distinctions are meaningful.

Let's backtrack a little: Mary got up early in the morning and went to the tomb in part because her heart was still broken over the death of Jesus. To make matters worse, the body of the One she loved was gone! She immediately ran for help. Peter and John didn't hesitate for even a moment; they headed straight for the tomb. (Please note that, although the passage doesn't name John, many theologians believe he was the "other disciple" who accompanied Peter. I share that belief.)

Jesus's disciples had been prepared for Jesus's death, burial, and resurrection because Jesus told them what was ahead. (See Luke 24:46.) However, He never said anything about what they would find in His tomb. He did not explain why the napkin would be found in a different place and condition from the rest of His grave clothes.

I have always wondered about the significance of these details. Over the years, many teachings have been offered. Some say the napkin was found, not folded, but twisted, because the cloth napkin was twisted and fastened to keep Jesus's jaw closed. Another teaching refers to a disputed Jewish custom regarding the dining practices of kings. According to this theory, a folded napkin signaled the king's intention to return and finish his meal. Those who favor this explanation believe the folded napkin is Jesus's signal that He is coming back. Whatever the meaning of the folded napkin and rumpled strips, we know this: He *will* return and gather us, His bride, to the feast of all eternity—the marriage supper of the Lamb!

As I preached on this subject, I turned around to Zack, the guitar player who played for the Crabb Family. He is a talented musician and an all-around in-tune kind of guy. I love the way he thinks. When I looked at him, there was excitement written all across his face. It was obvious that he had something he needed to say—and he unleashed it! He said, "Hey Jason, do you know why the grave clothes were wadded up in a place by themselves?"

I thought about it for a moment and realized that, although I was focused on the question of the napkin, I had not given much thought to the rest of the linens. I said, "No, Zack. Why?"

Zack's answer rang like a bell: "Because Jesus is finished with that!" When Zack said that, I got so excited I wanted to shout and dance all over the place. Jesus was done with His grave clothes. He was never coming back for them. What He did was done once and for all. He died for the sins of the world, and He would never have to do it again. His resurrection proved that His work was complete. Everything He had come to do was done. Death was finished.

All of the torment—being spit upon, cursed, having His beard plucked from His face, having spikes driven through His hands and feet, being beaten, suffocating on the cross, carrying the weight of the world's sin—all of it was over. Like Zack said, Jesus will never have to go back there. And if we accept His sacrifice, we won't have to go there either!

Paul told us as much. Led by the Holy Spirit, Paul left a message for the body of Christ. It ought to make us want to shout and dance from here into eternity.

> And if the Spirit of him who raised Jesus from the dead is living in you, he who raised Christ from the dead will also give life to your mortal bodies through his Spirit, who lives in you.
> —ROMANS 8:11

BACK TO THE POTTER'S WHEEL

The plan of redemption is a plan with a purpose. When we choose to be redeemed on the basis of the finished work of the cross, we place ourselves in God's kingdom and therefore in His care.

God's care is not a one-way street. He engages us, He interacts with us, and He leaves our free will intact. He has a plan for our spiritual development and for our overall well-being. That spiritual development brings us back to our earlier conversation about the Potter and the clay.

We did not and could not create ourselves. Likewise, when something about us is broken, we cannot fix ourselves. We can try to patch things up, tough it out, and get past the mayhem; but we cannot *restore* ourselves. We need God, and we need to tap into the fruit of redemption every single day. Doing so requires two things of us: trust and submission. We must trust God to lead us, provide for us, and heal us; we must also submit to His guidance and His plan.

Trusting God and accepting His will for us are twin aspects in the molding process we experience as believers. This process applies to every area of life, including our work. God places desires in our hearts. When we trust and submit to Him, they become our desires too. It starts with Him but continues in us. If we accept His plan, the question becomes, How diligently will we pursue those desires and perfect the gifts He has given us to fulfill those desires? That very question is at the heart of my advice to aspiring musicians when I tell them to practice, practice, practice.

Music has not been the only interest I have entertained over the course of my life, but it is the one constant that drives me. While I once aspired to be a basketball player, I have always desired, and still desire, to sing gospel music. I haven't had any formal training in music. I never took lessons or went to music school. I learned by doing. I practiced harmonies again and again until figuring out vocal parts became second nature. When I started playing bass and drums, I practiced until playing those instruments was a part of me. The same is true with guitar; I learned chords and riffs and have practiced them for years.

All of this learning is connected to a specific goal: to sing and play gospel music. There is more to it, however. The goal is not just to sing and play well. There is a larger ministry purpose involved. It involves the power of music and the way it can be used in the kingdom. I agree with the famous words of Martin Luther:

> Music is a fair and lovely gift of God....[It] drives away the Devil and makes people gay; they forget thereby all wrath, unchastity, arrogance, and the like....Experience proves that next to the Word of God only music deserves to be extolled as the mistress and governess of the feelings of the human heart.[2]

Music was created by God. Yet it is something we learn to do over time. All the practicing in the world won't produce results overnight. Results occur over the longer term; they are achieved through a steady diet of *becoming*. I know who I was created to be. I knew it at the Church of Philadelphia, but there was a process of development ahead. There still is. I believe with all my heart that God gave me these gifts, but I know it is up to me to pursue and develop them.

To acknowledge them and do nothing about them would have amounted to hiding my gifts under the proverbial bushel. (See Matthew 5:15, KJV.) Many, if not all, of the opportunities I have been blessed with would have passed me by. Worse, unless they were developed, my gifts could not have produced the fruit God intended. When my days were done, my gifts and me would have gone to the grave together.

That is not to say that I didn't have my moments when practicing was the last thing I wanted to do. Practicing can be frustrating and even boring. The fun part comes when you can see the results of practicing: when a song comes together, when a harmony soars, or when a song changes a life in front of your eyes. In those moments, all the years of practice seem like no trouble at all, and you can rejoice over all the endless scales you played!

Even when you are diligent to practice or study or do whatever it takes to excel in your calling, it is still not about how good you are. The issue is not what kind of voice you have or how well you can preach the Word. Instead, it is about being willing to cooperate and collaborate with God to the point that what He is after (the dream He has placed in your heart for His purposes) becomes reality.

Virtuosity and accolades are great, but in and of themselves they have no eternal value. Still, God encourages us through many avenues. It is all part of the molding process He uses to mature and guide us forward. One night on our bus some years ago, our keyboardist, Justin, and I were watching TV. There was a lot of talk at the time about possible nominations for the 2004 Grammy Awards. I made an off-the-cuff comment: "Wouldn't it be wild to see your name roll up and find out you were nominated for an award you didn't know about?" Neither Justin nor I thought about it any further. We were getting ready to sing at a church in Georgia at the time and went on with our business.

Then, out of the blue, my brother-in-law, Mike Bowling, stepped onto the bus. He seemed to be on a mission as he said, "Everybody sit down. I have something to tell you."

I gulped and thought someone must have been hurt.

"You're not going to believe this," Mike said, "but your album *The Walk* is nominated for a Grammy this year."

I assumed Mike was horsing around. I said, "I know you're kidding, but that's not a good joke." Still, Mike's *joke* was more than strange, because Justin and I had just joked about the Grammys for no apparent reason.

We were stunned to learn that Mike was not joking at all. The Crabb Family had been nominated for a Grammy. We Crabb kids were still young and had not been singing in larger venues for very long, so we could barely imagine such a possibility. We had worked hard and practically lived on that bus. We practiced as much as we could; I guess you could say we had paid our dues. In the end, however, the price we paid was nothing; it was the price Christ paid that mattered. He was the One who made all things possible.

We felt honored and privileged to be nominated. We didn't win, but it was an unforgettable experience, just the same. Little did I know that Grammy would come knocking again for my solo album. But that's a story for another chapter.

REAL-TIME COST

Receiving that first Grammy nomination created another, unexpected experience on the Potter's wheel.

When the time came for the awards ceremony, we went to Los Angeles, where all the hopefuls were gathered. It was a big deal for a Kentucky kid. From the red carpet to the events inside, we were surrounded by some of the most influential people in music. All kinds of music are represented; the place is a virtual "Who's Who" of every genre. Accomplished musicians, singers, songwriters, engineers, producers, comedians—anyone involved in the recording industry dreams of going to the Grammys.

It is quite a bash. Just being nominated for a Grammy is a miracle. Yet as happy an occasion as it would seem to be, I did not see much happiness on the faces of the artists gathered there. Instead, I saw a kind of unspoken misery. Big-name artists were decked out, bejeweled, coiffed, and put together like nobody's business. It was impressive. Yet there was something in their eyes that was sorrowful. I'm sure some were worried about losing; others were terrified of losing again; some were afraid of having to live up to their reputations if they won.

No one expressed any of these fears, but the inner turmoil was evident. I thought, "Man, these people don't know God's peace. They have become so centered on themselves and on who is going to win that there is no real joy in their being here."

It was heartbreaking. I was in a venue with some of the most talented people in the world. They seemed to have it all, yet they lacked peace, the one thing that makes everything else worthwhile. Even if they walked out with multiple Grammys, they would have gone home empty. They were in this thing alone, without the grace and mercy of God covering them and often without knowing who had given them their musical gifts.

At some point during the ceremonies, Donnie McClurkin was called to the stage to accept his Grammy. Donnie is a well-known gospel singer and a man I greatly admire not only as a musician but also as a believer and a man. I watched him as he proceeded to the stage to accept his award, and I listened intently as he did something I will never forget.

Instead of giving a fancy speech and talking about himself, Donnie asked the audience a question. He didn't dress up the question or try to play it cool. He just laid it out there and asked the audience, "How many Christians do we have in this house?"

We and many other believers screamed in response. As everyone else wondered where Donnie was going with this line of questioning, he said words to this effect: "I want to thank Jesus Christ, and I want to say that the Spirit of God is the One who got me this far. So I'm not about to shut up now."

Donnie's comments didn't make it on to the television broadcast; not all of the Grammy categories are aired. But we applauded his stand of faith in that hall. It was a bold move with a certain amount of risk attached to it. Not everyone appreciates public references to Jesus Christ. Some people think talking about Jesus makes you seem weird. Many people back away from those who proclaim His name. Some of those people are in a position to help your career.

Donnie was not worried about any of that. He did not care who had power or who didn't like what he said. He did not allow himself to be conformed to the venue, the event, or the lifestyles of the famous. He just spoke the truth to souls who needed to hear it. I don't know whether anyone took his words to heart or made a decision for Christ. I do know that because Donnie took the risk, every person in that auditorium had the opportunity to hear the very things they were dying to hear, whether they knew it or not. Donnie did his part; the rest was between them and God.

Donnie's words affected me deeply. He drew for me a line in the sand and gave me a brilliant example of how not to equivocate where my faith is concerned. The line he drew helped me to remember why compromise is not an option. If I stopped singing about Jesus and found ways to skirt around my faith, I could sing in more places, but I would forsake the One who paid the price for my gifts.

Donnie helped to clarify just how bad a choice that would be. I remember thinking, "I don't want to be another sad face in this crowd. I want to be the man Donnie McClurkin showed me. I am willing to pay that price. The rewards far outweigh the risks."

Therefore, I urge you, brothers, in view of God's mercy, to offer your bodies as living sacrifices, holy and pleasing to God—this is your spiritual act of worship. Do not conform any longer to the pattern of this world, but be transformed by the renewing of your mind. Then you will be able to test and approve what God's will is—his good, pleasing and perfect will.

—ROMANS 12:1–2

GOD'S AMAZING WAYS

That sea of pained faces at my first Grammy Awards ceremony reminds me that the world often sees Christianity in a distorted light. That is why our profession of faith is off-putting to so many people.

Some musicians might invite me to a session or some other event on the basis of my musicality but reject me for being a believer in Jesus Christ. I don't mean to (or want to) generalize; plenty of folks accept and respect my faith. I don't have a grab bag full of sob stories about being rejected in the industry. What I am saying is that a confession like Donnie's at the Grammys makes many people uneasy.

The reason is tied up in the world's view of Christianity. They tend to see Christianity as a laundry list of "thou shalts" and "thou shalt nots." As a result, some might see a person like me as a do-gooder who blindly follows a set of arbitrary rules, almost as though I had no mind of my own. I understand that point of view; it is one of the primary ways in which the enemy has fought Christianity for centuries. The devil doesn't deserve all the blame, however; sometimes we Christians present God in a similar light—not so much as a loving God who desires relationship with His children but as a finger-wagging, white-haired man who scares people into doing things His way.

People who shy away from the idea of relationship with God often fail to realize that God's commandments are based in His love for us. They see His *rules* as being designed to take the fun out of life. In reality, God's ways keep us from self-destructing; they lead us to what is in our best interests. And because Jesus's sacrifice paid the freight for our sins, doing things God's way is not drudgery. Once you understand the price that was paid in love for you, you desire to please the Savior and live a life of integrity under the protective hand of God.

That is the kind of life I live to sing about.

STUDY TO SHOW YOURSELF APPROVED

Even when we don't understand God and His ways, we are curious about Him. Mysteries always get our attention. We are drawn to them like moths to a flame. We love to solve the unknowns in life: What is going to happen next? How does the story end? Will this endeavor work out? Will I regret this decision a year from now?

For about a century now, Hollywood has capitalized on our obsession with the realm of the unknown, unsolved, or misunderstood. The world of science and technology is fueled by a similar passion, although with very different outcomes from the film industry. Scientists conduct research to solve problems. Their curiosity leads them to expand our body of knowledge and invent the things we need (and some we would be better off without).

The very curiosity that is part of our makeup as human beings helps us to learn and grow. We are born problem-solvers: put a riddle before us and we will search for the solution. Because we seek to understand things, we gain knowledge that can be applied to our everyday situations and lead to more questions.

History books are filled with the names of people who have applied themselves in this way. From Galileo to Florence Nightingale to Bill Gates, men and woman have sought to understand the mysteries of life and science and then apply what they learned to make for a better life.

Not everyone is as highly motivated as these innovators. In our spiritual lives, however, we are commanded by God to dig for answers. The Scriptures say, "Study to shew thyself approved unto God, a workman that needeth not to be ashamed, rightly dividing the word of truth" (2 Tim. 2:15, KJV).

The question is: Approved for what? I would answer this way: we need to be in practice, on our toes, ready to pass the tests we are sure to face. God wants us to succeed in the big quiz of life. He knows that if we experiment with man-made philosophies (however brilliant they seem to be), we will experience only momentary satisfaction, at best. In the end, our answers will not sustain us. If anything, they will further complicate our lives and break more things than they fix. The answers we need are in the living Word of God. They are the perfect answers God has provided for us.

Why is it called the *living* Word? Anything breathed by the Spirit is overflowing with life. We know that the Scriptures are God-breathed. (See 2 Timothy 3:16–17.) We also know that the Word contains thousands of promises made by God to us. These promises were made many centuries ago, before any of us were born, yet they apply to our lives. Many await manifestation.

Until a promise (that was made in the past) is manifested in your life, it remains ahead of you, somewhere in the future. Some kind of metamorphosis has to take place before that promise becomes a reality in the present. As you study the Word of God, His promises (and everything else His Word conveys) transform you. Often you can sense the change happening in your heart as you read your Bible. Yet the Scriptures also change you gradually, over time. The kind of change I am talking about is not just a change in thinking; it is a revolution in your being.

Only a *living* Word can create that kind of change. The price of our salvation was paid in full by Jesus Christ, who is the Word. One of the ways in which we *run* with the gift of life He gives is by studying God's Word. The rewards of this kind of diligence cannot be overstated. The Word of God is the strong rope that keeps us connected to our Anchor, Jesus Christ, and enables us to pass the big quiz of life.

SPEAK THE WORD

Have you noticed that it often takes a trial to get us to listen carefully for a word from God? I have. It seems that being reminded of our vulnerability keeps us humble. The older I get, the more I realize that Christianity is as much about knowing what you can't do without God as it is about rejoicing at what you can do because of Him!

Still, it is easy to become complacent, especially when everything is going well. I told you about the time we had a great sound check; I got excited about how well it went and assumed we would have a terrific concert. God shook me to my core and reminded me about

His role in the evening's *program*. He helped me get my priorities and perspective in order. I am glad that He did, although it felt anything but good that night.

Everything about Christianity involves looking beyond mere appearances. What we assume about God and about Christianity can get us into trouble. Those who continue to believe that God is motivated by anger or that Christianity is a set of rules and regulations will most likely continue to resist Him and miss out on a life they never imagined possible. For those of us who have known His love but make other assumptions about Him, we find ourselves all too often learning the truth the hard way.

Instead of knowing about God or what we think we know about Him, we are called to know Him deeply, as He really is. His Word helps us to know Him. He ordained the Scriptures to be written so we could *see* the invisible God. It should be our primary motivation for studying the Bible.

Yet we can study the Word until the South Pole looks like Honolulu and still not understand Him. How can that happen? By studying the Word as though it is a thing of the past, a wealth of information meant to be stored forever in the folds of our brains. I don't believe that He meant for His Word to be stockpiled inside us like steaks stacked in a freezer. Relationship with Him is not all about accumulating knowledge; it is about interacting with Him.

To do that, we have to keep it fresh and apply what we know in our daily walk, which is often a walk through the fire. The Bible minces no words in telling us that this life is a battle, not with people but with heavenly forces of darkness. Scripture tells us how to prepare for the fight and stay spiritually fit over the long haul.

We are to train up, muscle up, and stand up wearing the whole armor of God:

> For our struggle is not against flesh and blood, but against the rulers, against the authorities, against the powers of this dark world and against the spiritual forces of evil in the heavenly realms. Therefore put on the full armor of God, so that when the day of evil comes, you may be able to stand your ground, and after you have done everything, to stand. Stand firm then, with the belt of truth buckled around your waist, with the breastplate of righteousness in place, and with your feet fitted with the readiness that comes from the gospel of peace. In addition to all this, take up the shield of faith, with which you can extinguish all the flaming arrows of the evil one. *Take the helmet of salvation and the sword of the Spirit, which is the word of God.*
>
> —Ephesians 6:12–17, emphasis added

The sword of the Spirit mentioned in Ephesians 6:17 is an offensive weapon. We are to speak the Word of God and maintain the upper hand on the battlefield. The fact that God named His Word as part of our spiritual armor tells me that I need to use it. Yet God didn't just tell us about it; He also showed us how to use our sword. He gave us a perfect example through the life of Jesus.

After He was baptized in the Jordan River, Jesus spent forty days fasting in the wilderness. It was a pivotal time in His mission. His identity and purpose had been revealed in the plain sight of John the Baptist and his followers. Jesus would no longer be seen as just another carpenter from Galilee. The plan of redemption and the identity of the Redeemer had been leaked. Now that it was out in the open, Jesus knew the devil would attack with all of his might.

Sure enough, the devil showed up in the wilderness. Luke wrote that the devil went after Jesus throughout the forty days. Yet it was at the end of that period that we read of the devil's first tactical move. (See Luke 4:2–3.) He waited until Jesus was good and hungry and had been isolated from others for a long period of time. Assuming that his intended victim was in a weakened condition, Satan tried to derail Jesus and thwart His mission.

The devil used the same tactics He always uses: he tempted Jesus to follow *his* program instead of the Father's. Satan said, "If You are the Son of God, tell this stone to become bread" (Luke 4:3). In other words, "If You are who You say you are, why go hungry? Show me Your stuff, Jesus!"

After forty days without food, even a stale scrap of bread would look like a gourmet dish. Yet Jesus was not fooled by the devil's ploy. He did not allow Himself to be drawn into a discussion of His hunger or His power. Instead, He responded to the devil with the sword of the Spirit—the Word of God.

Jesus said, "It is written: 'Man does not live on bread alone'" (Luke 4:4). Jesus was quoting from Deuteronomy 8:3, which says, "[God] humbled you, causing you to hunger and then feeding you with manna, which neither you nor your fathers had known, to teach you that man does not live on bread alone but on every word that comes from the mouth of the Lord."

The devil is no match for the Word of God, yet he was not ready to give up. He tried to tempt Jesus again, this time offering Him the kingdoms of the world. (See Luke 4:6–7.) Jesus responded, saying,

"It is written: 'Worship the Lord your God and serve him only'" (Luke 4:8). Jesus's second response was another reference to God's Word; in this case, Jesus paraphrased Deuteronomy 6:13.

The devil is known for his persistence. In Luke 4:9–11, he took one more crack at Jesus's armor, daring Him to throw Himself down from the highest point of the temple so the angels would *catch* Him, as Psalm 91:11–12 promised.

Hungry and most likely weary from forty days of fasting, Jesus stayed suited up for battle. He dismissed the issue of whether or not the angels would come to His rescue and dealt with the larger issue of worship. He referred the devil to Deuteronomy 6:16, saying, "It says: 'Do not put the Lord your God to the test'" (Luke 4:12).

Jesus never lifted a finger; nor did He debate, deliberate, or get angry with the devil. He just picked up the sword of the Spirit and wielded it. The devil was soundly beaten. Luke wrote, "When the devil had finished all this tempting, he left him until an opportune time" (Luke 4:13). (Of course, the devil tempted Jesus in the wilderness precisely because he thought it would be an opportune time.)

How much more powerful is the sword of the Spirit now that we have Jesus Christ as our advocate with the Father? How confident can we be today, knowing that Jesus paid the biggest price of all and is interceding for us even now? (See Hebrews 7:25.) Think about it! We have a serious weapon to fight with! If the Word of God was good enough for Jesus to use, it is more than good enough for us!

Give It All to Jesus

So many issues can steal our attention and our strength. So many people share their struggles with me. Often they are dealing with serious situations that weigh heavily on their minds. They say things like, "You know, I'm dealing with this issue, and I don't know how to get out of it." Many say, "After all that's happened, I don't know how to forgive this person." Others are deeply wounded and say, "I was molested as a child. How can I get over that?"

The Bible says we have got to cast all of our cares and burdens upon Him. (See 1 Peter 5:7.) This command does more than offer us relief from the current storm; it tells us how to avoid taking on the bitterness that can develop and cause us greater problems in the future. God is saying, "Don't even think for a moment that you can handle this. I didn't create you to carry this problem or to live with hidden bitterness growing deep inside you. I created you to give it all to Me."

Bitterness is heavy, and it is poisonous. Unless it is rooted out, it will cause you to become someone you never imagined you would be. Our lives need not go that way, because Jesus already paid the price for us to be made whole. He bought your freedom and mine through His death and resurrection. Every promise He made is already ours, because He is trustworthy.

The greatest promise of all is found in Romans 10:13, which says, "Everyone who calls on the name of the Lord will be saved." Many people believe that the salvation spoken of in this verse is deliverance from sin alone. I believe there is much more to it than that. I believe that being saved means being saved from everything—from heartache, from pain and suffering, from torment of the mind—*everything*.

The price has been paid, yet wholeness is a process we need to embrace. We cannot earn salvation in any area. We cannot earn what has already been paid for. The work we are called to do is to take responsibility for our lives and refuse to blame others for our troubles. We must stay in the race and keep wearing our armor. Instead of hoping to survive the onslaught of the enemy, we need to have the attitude that says, "Jesus paid my way. I'll not surrender what He has promised me. I'm going to get through this battle and glorify Him!"

Today is the day to accept the deliverance for which He laid down His life.

Cast your cares on the LORD and he will sustain you;
he will never let the righteous fall.
—PSALM 55:22

CHAPTER 6

DIVINE HELP IN DESPERATE TIMES

He never offered our
victories without fighting

But He said help would
always come in time!

Mind-Boggling Grace

Victor Hugo's classic novel *Les Misérables* tells the unforgettable story of Jean Valjean, a thief imprisoned for stealing a loaf of bread and released years later to fend for himself. Because of his record, Valjean could find nowhere to stay until a kind bishop took him in and offered him the amenities of home.

Unused to kindness, Valjean thanked the bishop by stealing his silverware. The determined repeat offender was soon apprehended by police. He fully expected to be charged and thrown back in jail, but the bishop had something else in mind. In an act of grace and with an eye toward redemption, he gave Valjean a chance to make good in life. The clergyman told authorities the silverware had been given as a donation toward Valjean's new start. To bolster his story, he chided the ex-convict for leaving in haste without the silver candlesticks that were intended as part of the gift!

What a picture of grace! It reminds me of something Jesus said during His Sermon on the Mount:

> Do not resist an evil person. If someone strikes you on the right cheek, turn to him the other also. And if someone wants to sue you and take your tunic, let him have your cloak as well.
> —Matthew 5:39–40

Imagine suing someone for one million dollars in damages and having him offer you two million instead. Grace produces unexpected results and usually *arrests* its recipients. For sure, it takes me by surprise; I don't expect it or deserve it. Yet God chooses to give it freely. That is truly mind-boggling!

*[Jesus] said to me, "My grace is sufficient for you, for
my power is made perfect in weakness." Therefore I
will boast all the more gladly about my weaknesses, so
that Christ's power may rest on me.*

—2 CORINTHIANS 12:9

JOB FEARED GOD

One of the most famous Bible figures is Job. Most people (even those who have never opened a Bible) know something about Job. His life stands as a testament to the love that carries us through the fires of hardship and on to the place of redemption.

When things go terribly wrong in our lives or the lives of others, Job often comes to mind. We say things like, "Did you hear what happened to So-and-so? My Lord, she must have the patience of Job!"

Yet rarely does the world mention the brighter side of Job's life, which is just as much a part of his story. Job was a famously successful and prosperous man. He was highly regarded, respected, and powerful. As affluent as he was, he remained humble before God. As far as anyone could tell, Job had it all.

> In the land of Uz there lived a man whose name was Job. This man was blameless and upright; he feared God and shunned evil. He had seven sons and three daughters, and he owned seven thousand sheep, three thousand camels, five hundred yoke of oxen and five hundred donkeys, and had a large number of servants. He was the greatest man among all the people of the East.
>
> —JOB 1:1–3

God blessed Job with the very best in life. The things most people dream of were his. Yet Job's wealth was a small thing compared with his attitude toward God. Job worshiped God. His worship demonstrated his belief—his faith—that all good things come from God. Job's trust made him "blameless and upright" in God's eyes.

According to Job 1:3, Job "was the greatest man among all the people of the East." He owned seven thousand sheep, making Job a one-man wool industry. He had three thousand camels (the equivalent of having three thousand vehicles in your driveway). And what about Job's five hundred yoke of oxen and five hundred donkeys? For my granddad, it would have been like owning a thousand John Deere tractors.

God trusted Job with abundance. In a conversation with Satan, God bragged on Job, saying, "Have you considered my servant Job? There is no one on earth like him; he is blameless and upright, a man who fears God and shuns evil" (Job 1:8).

What higher compliment could a man receive than all-out affirmation from the Most High God? Yet Satan was not impressed. Instead he questioned Job's motives.

> Does Job fear God for nothing?…Have you not put a hedge around him and his household and everything he has? You have blessed the work of his hands, so that his flocks and herds are spread throughout the land. But stretch out your hand and strike everything he has, and he will surely curse you to your face.
>
> —JOB 1:9–11

God was not moved by Satan's accusations, because He knew Job's heart. He knew that even in the most desperate times, Job would stay true to His Maker. Satan disagreed and was determined to prove God wrong.

Job's suffering was about to begin.

JOB'S DESPERATE DAYS

Satan had God's permission to try Job's soul, and he tried it with a vengeance. He killed Job's children and destroyed Job's livestock. (See Job 1:13–19.) Job was rocked to his very core. He could not understand why such tragedy had befallen his family. Yet he knew that God was good, trustworthy, and worthy of his worship, even in the worst of times.

> At this, Job got up and tore his robe and shaved his head. Then he fell to the ground in worship and said: "Naked I came from my mother's womb, and naked I will depart. The LORD gave and the LORD has taken away; may the name of the LORD be praised." In all this, Job did not sin by charging God with wrongdoing.
>
> —JOB 1:20–22

Job suffered many setbacks during his days of desperation. He endured physical trials, strife in his marriage, and the accusations of his *friends*. There were days when he despaired of life and longed for the grave, but Job never forsook God. Instead he pressed through the struggle, hung in with God, and ended up more blessed than he had ever been.

> The LORD blessed the latter part of Job's life more than the first. He had fourteen thousand sheep, six thousand camels, a

thousand yoke of oxen and a thousand donkeys. And he also had seven sons and three daughters.

—JOB 42:12–13

Before his misery, Job was a man with high expectations of good things. After suffering much hardship and a complete reversal of fortune, Job came to a point in his life when he began to expect the worst.

Except for God's mercy and grace!

Job eventually saw a complete turnaround from the worst possible circumstances to the best ones imaginable. Although it looked like Job was finished, although there were times when he wished he had never been born, Job lived to see better days.

You may be in the midst of desperate times right now. You may have climbed out of bed this morning wishing you hadn't. It may look as though nothing will ever change for the better. I can remember a time when it looked that way to me. Yet God proved me wrong. There were *much better* days ahead—and there are for you too.

No matter the situation, one thing is certain: our Redeemer lives! (See Job 19:25.) His grace can carry you over every obstacle, even when lifting your finger is more than you can manage.

TINY AS A MUSTARD SEED

I don't understand how God's grace works; I just know that it does and that faith is involved. Faith is the kind of *knowing* that is central to how the kingdom of God operates. We don't have to understand *how* things will change for the better. We are not called to figure out *how* God will meet our need. We don't have to stay up nights imagining which scenario will make an uptick out of a downturn. All we have to do is believe that "with God all things are possible" (Matt. 19:26).

I won't kid you: there are moments when I lose sight of this truth. Sometimes I forget to factor His grace into whatever situation I am facing. At times my anchor shakes loose, and I drift far enough downstream that my inadequacy haunts me. When I ride that part of the river, it becomes difficult to look beyond my shortcomings and see God's sufficiency. When I buy into my insecurities, my doubt looks bigger than my faith. Left unchecked, doubt can gain the upper hand in my mind. It might be a momentary tussle, or it might drag on for weeks.

This happened not long ago after my family quit touring together. I got to a place where I felt the weight of the world on my shoulders. Stepping out into a *solo* ministry meant taking on a lot of additional responsibility and expense.

Transitions, even those that lead to better things, can be treacherous. The enemy knows that if you lose sight of God's grace, worry will eat your lunch! That is exactly what happened to me. The joy of my new path had begun to evaporate in the face of what I saw as insurmountable obstacles to the mission. I still had God's confirming word tucked in my heart, I still wore Pastor Parsley's watch as a symbol of what God had said, and I still desired to sing gospel music and preach God's Word. But my words became negative. Before I knew it, I was feeling like a world-class sad sack. I was so worried about all that needed to be done that I set my faith—however much of it there was—on the back burner. Like Job, my sense of expectation was trained on the wrong details; instead of seeing the amazing road ahead, I focused on all the rocks in my path.

Thank God I have a wife who loves me enough to read me the riot act. Shellye took me to the back of the bus one night and said, "Honey, I'm sick of hearing you whine, and I'm tired of watching you mope around. You need to look at what God has already done."

Shellye was right. She didn't tell me what I wanted to hear; she told me what I needed to hear. She brought faith back to the forefront so that God's grace could operate in my life. I had turned the whole thing upside down. I was trying to carry God's part of the ministry—the provision, logistics, worries about personnel, and all the other things I could not *make happen* through my own efforts. As a result, I was exhausted and discouraged and unable to do my rightful part.

Shellye's words catapulted me back on track. My perspective shaped up, and I remembered what I had seemed to forget: we were not created to live under the circumstances. We are not called to pump up our faith until it is *big enough* to take us through the fire. We just have to use the faith we have, and He will make something big of it. Jesus said it this way:

> I tell you the truth, if you have faith as small as a mustard
> seed, you can say to this mountain, "Move from here to there"
> and it will move. Nothing will be impossible for you.
> —MATTHEW 17:20

The measure of faith is not a matter of how much you have, but of what you do with it. Faith the size of the tiniest seed is more than enough. That is evident in Jesus's choice of words: "You can say to this *mountain*, 'Move...' and it will move" (emphasis added).

Move a mountain? Heck, my troubles weren't *that* big! When God called me to strike out on my own, He didn't ask me to relocate Mount

Hood. And even if He had, my prospects for success would not have been tied to how I felt or how clear my path was at the time.

The idea of grace is that our success is not based in performance. It is based on His ability to accomplish what He has ordained. All we need to do is plant our tiny seeds of faith and keep on walking, believing that God is God. He will see us through whatever it is— even the fire itself—one day at a time.

A Legacy of Faith

Mustard-seed faith is part of my family heritage. I am so thankful for it. Many storms have crossed our paths, but that faith has always prevailed. I have seen my loved ones' faith move so many mountains that I would not know where to begin to share the examples that have affected my life.

I have been inspired by everyone from parents to siblings to in-laws and grandparents. My grandma is one of those people who know just how to water the faith seed. She has had lots of practice over many years, and always she has given the rest of us a good example to follow.

Except when she's needed to give me a strong dose of correction, Grandma always calls me *Jace*. She'll call and say, "Jace, I woke up at two thirty this morning and had you on my mind, so I started praying for you."

I'll think back to the night before and say, "Grandma, that's about the time we had a blowout on the bus."

Grandma has done this many times. I know she is praying for me and the rest of us, Bible in hand. I may never know until I get to heaven how many times she has prayed us out of danger or difficulty. I do know this: Grandma can pray anyone through the fire.

During Granddad's last days, when he was confined to bed and ready to leave this earth, Grandma remained by his side. On the morning he died, she stayed in the bedroom with him virtually every moment. Other family members were there too. When Grandma went inside to get a drink of water, Granddad began gasping for breath. He knew it was time for him to go, so he motioned for everyone to get Grandma.

Grandma knew the love of her life was about to leave her. She grabbed Granddad's hand, kissed him on the forehead, and said, "Lee, I love you."

He tried to say that he loved her too, but was unable to speak. Grandma knew exactly what he was saying. Even in the face of traumatic loss—even knowing she was about to be widowed— Grandma's faith undergirded her emotions. In their final moments together, she kept her focus on her husband and made sure his departure reflected the love they shared.

She said, "If you see Jesus, you go on and be with Him." Then my little red-haired country grandmother comforted Granddad in her usual spunky way with her down-home dialect, saying, "I'll be behind you directly."

After Granddad took his last breath, Grandma threw her hands in the air and began to pray in the language that she prayed best. She had just been separated from her mate, but Grandma had the joy of knowing his life had ended well and he was home in heaven. As she prayed in the Spirit, the room filled with peace. Because of Grandma's mustard-seed faith, her own prayers ushered Granddad on into glory.

We all miss Granddad terribly, but we know he could not have asked for a better homegoing. My grandmother still lives in the house Granddad built with his own hands. It's small, but it stands out; Granddad painted it a Smurf shade of blue. It is probably the only blue house in the area. Grandma misses Granddad every day, but she still has a lot to live for. She takes life one step at a time and gives every day to the Lord.

Grandma is a woman of faith if ever I saw one.

Pure, Unadulterated Trust

God is trustworthy—100 percent trustworthy in every situation. When we lose sight of His greatness, we mentally and emotionally magnify our adversity. That is what happened to me when I went through the down days I mentioned earlier. I faced real challenges, but they were signs of God's blessing. He was opening new doors and taking me to new places in life. I should have been jumping for joy, but because my perspective was skewed, I felt down in the dumps instead.

When you keep issues in the proper perspective, there is no limit to where trust in God can take you. Some time ago, we were made aware of an almost incredible, fully documented testimony about a boy from Oklahoma. The child was involved in a horrific accident with a four-wheeler. The vehicle flipped over onto him and crushed every bone in his face, leaving him in a coma for twenty-six days.

The child's situation was desperate. Doctors held out no hope for his survival. Everyone who knew him was devastated. He came from a strong Christian family and was a preacher's kid. His family loved

God and served Him. You can imagine the questions rolling around in everyone's mind: "Oh, God, why this? How could this happen?"

Many people prayed for the boy to recover. Miraculously, and to the amazement of his doctors, he survived. Once he became conscious, his father asked him to share what he had experienced. The boy said that while he was comatose he heard these lyrics (from "Through the Fire"): "...help will...come time." As young and broken as he was—even unable to move or speak—he trusted God and believed the help he needed was coming!

Help did come, and right on time. The boy's precious life was preserved against all odds. The battle was not over, however. A long road of recovery lay ahead. The child's injuries were life changing. He had no functioning jaw. His esophagus was damaged so that he could not swallow anything without drowning. Eating normally was out of the question, so he had to be fed through a tube. His facial bones were so shattered that doctors had to use some of his ribs to re-create a jaw structure. His new jaw was a great miracle, but he had no teeth and no prospects of any new teeth growing in.

Except for God's grace! After a period of time, the boy went for a checkup. The doctor was floored by what he saw: teeth were growing out from the transplanted ribs that formed the boy's new jaw. Not only that, but the ribs now missing from his chest had been replaced with new ones that had grown in their place!

God was still not done. After five or six years without being able to swallow or eat, the boy heard someone singing "Through the Fire" at church. He began walking around the altar as he listened intently to the song. Then God spoke to him and said, "You can eat tomorrow."

You can imagine what exciting news that was. The implications of being able to eat were enormous. By faith, the boy believed that God had spoken, and he hung on to what God said. Even after so many experiences with choking (and the prospects of choking to death), the boy acted on God's promise and ate the very next day. He has been eating ever since and has shared his testimony countless times.

Traveling the way I do, I get to hear so many testimonies that encourage me in faith and in ministry. Not long ago, a pregnant woman shared a very sad report: doctors told her that her unborn child would not survive. It was devastating news to bear; it broke our hearts just hearing it. We stopped the service right then and there. We prayed for the woman and her baby and asked God to divinely heal the child.

After that service, we went on our way, not knowing the outcome of the woman's pregnancy. The next time we were in her city, she brought her baby to the service and testified that the Lord had healed the child in the womb! Another woman stood up. She had been told by doctors that her unborn baby was going to die. We prayed for her, and guess what? The Lord healed her baby too!

This world is full of trouble. There are situations in every corner of the globe that defy explanation and seem beyond hope. None of them is bigger than God. When trouble comes, I am thankful for my favorite scripture on trust:

> Trust in the LORD with all your heart and lean not on your own understanding; in all your ways acknowledge him, and he will make your paths straight.
>
> —PROVERBS 3:5–6

WALK IN HIS COMMANDMENTS

Leaning on your own understanding means operating in what you know instead of what God knows. When I sense something about my path becoming crooked, I know I need to backtrack to where I started leaning on my understanding instead of His. For sure, I want to avoid a path that is heading the wrong way. I don't want to do damage control at the end of the mess. I would rather let God make my path straight right here and now.

In chapter 5, we talked a little about the true nature of God's commandments. The Bible tells us that He is a just God, not a mean God. He wants the best for us, so He provides explicit instructions that enable us to live well. His commandments warn us against certain practices and beliefs. They also make clear which practices and beliefs He wants us to embrace. More than anything, God loves us and wants to keep us from defeat and destruction.

Today's society, for the most part, reflects the world's rebellion against every commandment of God. Five minutes in front of your television will tell you that. Adultery is seen as a popular alternative to fidelity and the sacrifice purity entails. Disrespect has become a sign of being savvy and street-wise. Independence has become proof of inner strength.

Look online or in the newspaper where hot-button issues are displayed in black and white. Arguments over the sanctity of life are made as though the preciousness of life were debatable. Freedom of worship is discussed as though it were contrary to our founding principles. Violence and idolatry are everywhere.

Fear God, and keep his commandments: for this is the whole duty of man. For God shall bring every work into judgment, with every secret thing, whether it be good, or whether it be evil.

—ECCLESIASTES 12:13–14, KJV

The world has become distorted, not because we long for misery but because we lose sight of God's love for us. It happened way back in the Garden of Eden. Adam and Eve knew enough not to eat from the tree of the knowledge of good and evil. They accepted the warning as part of the ideal life they had been given by God. They honored God's command and enjoyed the benefits of His guidance.

It all worked perfectly until the serpent deceived Eve about God's love. He told Eve, "God knows that when you eat of [the tree] your eyes will be opened, and you will be like God, knowing good and evil" (Gen. 3:5). Eve fell for the devil's sleight of hand. They lost sight of God's love, disobeyed His command, and suffered the consequences.

The world has followed in their footsteps ever since. Some of the smartest people on the planet have been deceived just as Eve was— and just as we all are at times. As a result, people discount God's love. They see His commandments as being irrelevant to their lives. They are caught unawares by the destruction that lawlessness wreaks.

I fell into that trap as a youth. It could have cost me my life—but for the grace of God.

It Comes Down to Choices

Every moment of every day we are choosing something: to believe or deny, to give or withhold, to act or remain passive, to tell the truth or a lie. When we drill down to the bedrock of our choices, they are more profound than we realize: what we are really deciding is whether we will serve God and His kingdom or Satan and the kingdom of darkness. It is exactly as Joshua told his people: "Choose for yourselves this day whom you will serve.... But as for me and my household, we will serve the LORD" (Josh. 24:15).

That is a potent statement, so let me clarify: I'm not talking about choosing which pair of shoes to wear or what kind of birthday cake to buy (although, if God gives you direction in those things, go ahead and follow). I'm talking about the conduct of our lives overall and where that conduct takes us. There is no disputing that the right choices end up very differently than the wrong ones.

When God's love is in the front of our minds, we make better choices, and we find it easier to do so. When we allow circumstances to obscure that love, things can go haywire in a hurry. They did for me. There were moments when the outcome was up for grabs. Thankfully, God got my attention, but it took awhile until I was out of the woods.

It started during my teens after my parents were divorced. Our home life changed just as I entered the age where I wanted to throw off the restraint of my parents. I did not want to be under anyone's thumb. I wanted to make my own way in life.

Most teens experience these feelings on some level. They are not children anymore, but they are not adults, either. They realize they can exercise more control over their lives because they are not as dependent as they once were. Too often they find self-destructive ways to exert their independence. For me, the divorce provided an excuse to rebel. The desire to rebel was already working inside me, but now I had found just enough leeway to walk it out.

The choices I made were bad choices. I started running with the wrong crowd. It wasn't like I didn't know better. I grew up in church. I was raised in the Word and prayer. Yes, things were tough. The two people I loved most in the whole world had separated. I wasn't sure how to get through that. Still, my parents had taught me well. I knew right from wrong. I knew that in the end I would be judged for what I *did* not what *they did.*

Not realizing my own immaturity, I tried to become my own man. I opened myself up to things that I did not understand. I began experimenting with drugs. This might be the hardest thing of all to share publicly. I have done it before, but I need to tell the story here. Millions of teens fall into unfortunate circumstances. Many of them try to ease their pain and drown their sorrows with a cheap high. They look for ways to prove themselves. The choices they make are loaded with danger. If sharing my story can help one young person set himself or herself right, that is all that matters.

We lived in a poor neighborhood where drugs were cheap. It is amazing how easy the devil will make it for you to destroy yourself. One day I was out in the woods by myself trying a drug I had done before. As I sat on a stump, I started to feel high. The next thing I knew, demons came up out of the ground. That is exactly what I saw. It was terrifying. The little demons moved toward me. The closer they came, the greater my awareness that my life was spinning out of control. Whatever control I thought I had was now given over to the enemy—and I did not know how to get it back.

One of the scariest things about substance abuse is the realization that you are under the influence of someone or something that can destroy you. Seeing those demons engraved that reality into my psyche. As they continued to approach, an almost overwhelming fear came over me, and I fell off the stump.

In an instant, I became sober. It was as though I had not taken anything at all! I really believe the entire experience was a warning from God, a kind of *scared straight* moment for which I am thankful. That day could have ended very differently. I believe Satan fully intended to take me out. I could easily have died of an overdose. Any number of scenarios could have ended my life while I was in that condition.

Afterward I could not help but wonder what kind of heartache my parents and siblings would have endured if I had died. I thought about the repercussions on people in the community or those with whom I grew up in church. The legacy I would have left would have fallen far short of what God had in mind.

I am so grateful that no worst-case scenarios played out. I am grateful to my family for praying me through. I know that the years of prayer from Grandma on down played a role in my deliverance that day. Looking back, it is clear that even though my heart had cooled toward God, the things I learned at home and in church held. I still thought about the things Jesus said during His earthly walk. As I wandered off the path, some of His words struck me more than others. His statement recorded in Mark 9:47–48 hit me hard: "And if your eye causes you to sin, pluck it out. It is better for you to enter the kingdom of God with one eye than to have two eyes and be thrown into hell, where 'their worm does not die, and the fire is not quenched.'"

What an intense passage that is. The second half of it was a quote from Isaiah 66:24. The idea of mutilating yourself to avoid the wrath of hell is pretty strong stuff. The idea of going to hell, where "the worm does not die" is stronger still. Although the Hebrew and Greek words for "worm" in this case literally mean "maggot,"[1] the idea is said to involve the endless torment of the human conscience living on in hell. The "worm" is a picture of the consuming memory of sins committed during life.[2] The image was enough to rattle my cage.

As I skated close to the edge, I developed a sense of my own mortality. I wanted no part of hell or hellish outcomes. I did not want to look back over my life with regret for every time I had ignored the convicting move of the Holy Spirit. I did not want to remember every service I attended and every sermon I heard preached as another missed opportunity. The last thing I wanted was to continue making choices in opposition to the will of God.

God gave me a chance to get back to Him. He delivered me from drugs. That was the beginning of the rest of my life. But there was still plenty of healing to be done.

THE GRACE OF DIVINE PROTECTION

There were things I had to learn and some that I needed to forget forever. As turbulent as my life was, I came to the realization that I was still in control of my decisions. It would have been easy to blame other people for my problems, but it would have been dishonest. I was the one who chose to step out from under the protection of

God's love and commands. I chose to dabble in a lifestyle I knew was wrong. The Bible says that all of us are tempted and God gives all of us a way out of temptation:

> No temptation has seized you except what is common to man. And God is faithful; he will not let you be tempted beyond what you can bear. But when you are tempted, he will also provide a way out so that you can stand up under it.
> —1 Corinthians 10:13

He did that for me. He showed me the real issue in my life. I had become bitter about so many things. That bitterness was forming a choke hold on my life. God knew that and made a way of escape, one that I would understand. My experience in the woods got my full attention. It was the beginning of my getting back to where I had started with God.

In order to heal, I had to let go of the junk dragging me down. I needed God's help to do that. One of the lifelines He threw me was music. Not very long after this experience, He began to draw me closer to Himself through song. I found fulfillment in worshiping Him. I found pleasure in using my creative gifts to glorify His name and not my own. I looked forward to our family times of ministry.

Being in that realm—on the road, on the platform, and on the road again—kept me focused on the right things. God used all of it to heal my heart and straighten out the crooked parts of my path. My heart softened, and the bitterness fell away. And all the while, God was fulfilling His plan for my life.

Had God not intervened in those desperate times, I don't know what would have happened. I know this much: if I had kept moving away from God, I would have made a common, very human mistake. Instead of taking responsibility for my actions, I would have allowed the tough times to become the cornerstone of the rest of my life. I would have added more cracked bricks to that faulty foundation and would have become even more bitter when my life came crashing down later.

It happens all the time. In fact, I am writing a song about the way we tend to stay in the places of our hurt. We feed that broken frame of mind by meditating on all the bad things that have happened. If we are not careful to choose our thoughts along God's ways of thinking, we begin to tell ourselves, "I am the way I am because of what happened to me back then."

That mind-set is music to the enemy's ears. He is the ultimate opportunist and will gladly bake up a truckload of bad bricks and then help you pile them on. He will feed your mind-set morning, noon, and night if you let him. His mission is *to take you out*. The more help you give him, the happier he is.

That is the harsh reality and the tough-love message I minister to young people to this day. I share with them the lesson I learned on the backside of my brief experimentation with drugs: no matter what we go through in life, no matter how many lemons life throws at us, God will teach us how to respond. He knows that some things are out of our control. I had no control over my parents' breakup. It happened, and there was nothing I could do to change it. My responsibility began with choosing how to react to the situation. That was the part for which God would hold me accountable.

The greatest gift God has given us is the power of choice. We can better our lives, or we can make matters worse. I thank God for helping me through the hard times and sparing my life by His mercy and grace. I thank Him for watching over me and protecting me the way He did. I'm especially thankful that my life didn't end that day in the woods. There was so much living yet to do—so much I would have missed and so much I would have withheld from others just by leaving.

As hard as it is to talk about this period of my life, I am so glad that God gave me this opportunity to share it with you. I pray that His purposes are fulfilled in it.

CHAPTER 7

REFUSING TO GIVE IN
TO THE ENEMY

*Just remember when you're
standing in the valley of decision*

*And the adversary
says, "Give in!"*

SATAN PLAYS FOR KEEPS

IN THE CONTEXT of eternity, this earthly life is short—amazing, but short. All too easily, we become engrossed in exhausting thoughts about what has happened or what has not. Without realizing it, we allow our regrets to root us in the past. Before we know it, the future has come and gone.

That is the devil's grand scheme. He arranges skirmishes right and left. Health issues arise. The kids get off track. Marriage woes creep in. Finances become frayed. While we work to put out the fires, we become nearsighted. We lose sight of the enemy's true intent.

The devil is a master of strategy. He is not really after your health, your children, your marriage, or your finances. What he really wants is your faith. He knows that if he can rob you of that most precious asset, he will be able to derail your thinking, your doing, and your calling. If he runs the play just right, he can rob you of your will to live.

Satan fights dirty and plays for keeps. Those are the raw facts. He played dirty when he tempted Jesus in the wilderness. He seized an opportunity (knowing Jesus had been fasting for forty days) and distorted the Word and will of God. Satan intended to derail the mission of Christ. He failed miserably. (See Matthew 4.) It wasn't the last defeat he would suffer at the hands of Jesus: the Resurrection would finish the job. From that day, Satan lost the fight where God's people are concerned!

I can almost hear you ask, "How did Satan lose? I have been through so much. My family and friends have been through so many ordeals. Where is the victory in that?"

Do you remember the woman I wrote about earlier, the woman who had an incurable disease? She was up against it in a big way. Her health was in jeopardy; she lacked insurance; she had a family to feed; she was in fear of losing her job. Yet she said something that spoke of victory. She started a new job because she knew she had to get back to living.

She was tired of sitting around doing nothing. She was through letting the devil run roughshod over her. She took back the reins and decided to go with God, even if it cost her. I like that about her! So many things had gone wrong in her life, and she had more than her fair share of regrets. Nonetheless, she made a choice to move forward. She had the guts to look the downside in the eyes and fight. She was not willing to crawl under the covers and let depression roll over her. She was not about to give the enemy that ground. She resisted the power of darkness and refused to hand over control of her future.

There was another thing about that woman that lit the fire of my hope: she said she was hanging on to every word the preacher said. She was taking hold of life—the real life found in the Word of God.

When you hang on to His Word and apply the Scriptures to your life, you can't help but live. You *have to* live! The Word of God is life itself. This is true no matter what is happening around you or to you. Even if you experience failure on every front or those closest to you fail you miserably or your retirement fund fails or unexpected difficulties arise—whatever happens, the answers and the healing you long for are found in God's Word.

When you start believing what the Word says about you, about God, and about your future, there is only one possible outcome: life will rise up within you. First John 5:4 says that "everyone [who is] born of God overcomes the world. *This is the victory* that has overcome the world, even our faith" (emphasis added).

The devil is no match for God or His Word!

The thief comes only to steal and kill and destroy; I have come that they may have life, and have it to the full.
—JOHN 10:10

DOING NOTHING EQUALS GETTING NOTHING

There is an Old Testament story from the days of Elisha that explains a key element of victory. That element is *action*; you have to take what you believe and act on it. Thinking about it is the start. Talking about it greases the wheels. But doing it—that is where the rubber meets the road.

If you do nothing, you can expect nothing to change. This was certainly true for Israel in ancient times. One of its most difficult periods came in Elisha's day when Samaria was besieged by the Arameans. Turmoil and fear were the order of the day. Food prices were so severely inflated that eating became a luxury most people could not afford. Famine set in. Conditions were so extreme that mothers cannibalized their own children. There was no relief in sight. Aware of the people's fate, the king tore his garments in distress. (See 2 Kings 6:24–30.)

Even the strongest people in Samaria were at risk of harm or starvation. The young, the old, and the sick were more vulnerable. Lepers, who were isolated and rejected in the best of times, faced dismal prospects. Yet in the middle of the siege, four lepers looked death in the eye and decided to do *something*. What they did changed *everything*.

> There were four men with leprosy at the entrance of the city gate. They said to each other, "Why stay here until we die? If we say, 'We'll go into the city'—the famine is there, and we will die. And if we stay here, we will die. So let's go over to the camp of the Arameans and surrender. If they spare us, we live; if they kill us, then we die."
>
> At dusk they got up and went to the camp of the Arameans. When they reached the edge of the camp, not a man was there, for the LORD had caused the Arameans to hear the sound of chariots and horses and a great army....So they got up and fled in the dusk and abandoned their tents...horses...and donkeys. They left the camp as it was and ran for their lives.
>
> —2 KINGS 7:3–7

In the valley of decision, the lepers made a calculation: "If we sit here, we will starve for sure. Entering the city will be no better. Only the Arameans have food. If we surrender to them, they will either feed us or kill us. Either way, it's better than sitting here and dying a slow death. What have we got to lose?"

The lepers understood a simple equation: *doing nothing equals getting nothing*. If they had lingered at the city gate, it would have been a matter of time until their bones were all that remained of them. The situation was as dire as it could be. So, they took a step forward. It was risky, but at least it was a step.

The result was supernatural. God brought a complete turn-around, not just for them but for Israel. Fearing for their lives, the Arameans fled, leaving food, silver, clothing, animals, and everything else behind. The lepers entered the camp unopposed, took their fill, and alerted the king. A great bounty was recovered and food prices came down! (See 2 Kings 7:8, 11–16.)

OVERCOMING PASSIVITY

I don't know about you, but I sometimes find myself sitting at the gate, neither in nor out but somewhere in between. It is uncomfortable and uninspiring, but I hang out there just the same, lazy and satisfied with where I'm at with Christ. The longer I sit there, the worse I feel, because doing nothing is not a neutral choice. If you are not moving forward, you are sliding backward. It is a form of death—the slow death of spiritual starvation.

The story of the lepers encourages me. Anyone watching their situation would have agreed that these men had nothing going for them. Yet they had gumption. They refused to remain passive. They put their lives on the line and made a difference by making the first move.

The lepers did their part, and God did what only He can. He went out ahead of them and turned a fierce fighting force into an army of *chickens*. He caused them to hear a sound that turned the tables in the conflict. Against all odds, four lepers marched into the enemy's camp and were the first to plunder it.

Please don't misunderstand me: making the first move does not mean taking foolish or impulsive steps that cut against the grain of God's ways. What I am talking about is being proactive in your faith and moving toward His will and provision for you. If you will press through life's difficulties and take that first step forward, God will go before you and turn the tide in your favor.

The same is true in a purely spiritual sense. If you feel like you are drying up in the place you are at, if it seems like you are dying inside, take a tip from the four lepers. Make that first step. Hop off the gate, and search out what He wants and has for you. Read the Word of God. Glean fresh hope and inspiration from His promises. Take nourishment and courage from the love He expresses through His Word.

Then make a move.

STAY IN TUNE WITH GOD

My siblings and I grew up in the Church of God, a full-on full gospel denomination that prays with passion and believes that God will answer. Whenever someone was sick, someone else would break out the oil, anoint the sick person, and pray for healing. Worship was vibrant. There was a free-flowing atmosphere of praise. Our church was more in tune to the Holy Spirit than to a fixed program. No two services were the same. You never knew 100 percent where things would end up.

That upbringing affects my life to this day. I rarely have a fixed set list for concerts. We decide on a song or two to start with and then see where the Spirit leads. He knows better than we do what He has in mind. He understands perfectly what the needs are and how to meet them. I love to watch where He takes us and what He does. It is a new adventure every time.

Our church background still affects our family too. My grandmother is a little Pentecostal lady who recognizes the presence of the Lord and just flows with Him. For years now it has been hard for her to walk, but when the power of God hits her, watch out. She will tear up the floor! It is a sight to behold. First, she starts out moving her hands, and before you know it, she's making sounds like a siren going off. That's when I tell everybody, "You'd better duck, because Grandma's bobby pins are fixing to fly. Pretty soon, they'll be in you or the drywall, one or the other."

Grandma never gives in to the enemy. I've told you about her middle-of-the-night prayers. I know she had a lot to do with my coming out of my teens in one piece. She is not one to look at the situation and throw up her hands in despair. That's just not Grandma. In fact, I am convinced that even if her legs failed her completely she would find a way to get up and shout God's praises! Her secret is that she stays in tune with God. Her connection with Him keeps her from quitting. She has put all her eggs in her *God basket* and never tries to sneak one back out.

I thank God for my upbringing. The things we learned at home and in church have sustained us over the years through all kinds of situations.

In 2003 we were asked to sing "Through the Fire" at the Dove Awards ceremony in Nashville. I can't tell you how much that invitation meant to my family. It is an honor, and every Christian artist's dream, to be asked to perform at the Dove Awards! There is not time enough in the program for everyone to play, and there were plenty of talented folks to choose from—artists I had admired, in some cases, since childhood. It was a *big deal*. Little did I know what a challenge it was going to be.

I rarely have problems with my voice, but the day before the awards ceremony, I could barely speak above a whisper. I had laryngitis for the Dove Awards! The question "Why, God?" leapt to center stage in my mind. I remember thinking, "This is shaping up to be a train wreck. I can't think of a worse time to lose my voice!"

The only hope I had was God. It was a perfect opportunity to pray and trust Him. I did my part; I rested my voice as much as I could. Nothing seemed to help. I knew there was no way I would be able to sing the song without God touching me. I told Him as much. I prayed and asked Him to help me sing the song the same way I had sung it in church or any other venue.

When we stepped on the stage, it was clear just how much I needed God. Singing may come naturally to me, but a human voice is a human voice. It has its ups and downs. Singers get laryngitis sometimes. Unless you can look to God, you might as well call off the engagement.

From the stage I looked out into the audience. Everyone I could think of was there. I remember Kirk Franklin smack dab on the front row. My mind wanted to run wild with worry about just how badly this could turn out, yet we had done all we could do. We prayed and we showed up. And just as sure as the sky is blue, God went ahead of us!

No sooner did the first note sound than God's anointing hit that place. Nothing mattered but Him. Not my throat. Not my voice. Not the performance. It was all about Him. And did He ever show up!

Laryngitis and all, I sang the song just like I had sung it hundreds of times before. It was not a train wreck; it was an authentic *God moment*. By the power of the Holy Spirit, the song ministered to everyone in that crowd, including us. Ironically, we received more positive feedback about "Through the Fire" that night than we had ever received before.

If Grandma had been there, I am sure she would have danced!

> *Whatever you ask for in prayer , believe that you have received it, and it will be yours.*
>
> —MARK 11:24

FEAR THE LORD ONLY

Solomon wrote, "The fear of the LORD is the beginning of knowledge: but fools despise wisdom and instruction" (Prov. 1:7, KJV). The fear of the Lord helps us to stay on the straight path. It is one of the ways He protects us from getting into foolishness.

Despising wisdom and instruction is rebellion. When children shrug off their parents' counsel, they rebel against something they don't really understand. They believe that the rules are designed to make their lives miserable. They don't recognize their own vulnerability. They have not developed an awareness of the things their parents see lurking in the shadows. Often instead of honoring their parents, they hold them in disdain. As children of God, we sometimes do the same thing.

The fear of the Lord involves reverence for Him.[1] It is not a fear of knowing Him or inviting Him into your affairs. It is not a crippling fear or a sense that He is waiting to strike you with lightning the moment your tongue or your foot slips. The fear of the Lord is the awareness of all He is and means to you. This reverence recognizes His love. It sees both His awesomeness and His grace, His judgment and His mercy. The fear of the Lord acknowledges that all honor is due Him, in all things.

The fear of the Lord is the right kind of fear to have. Other kinds of fear—the fear of life, death, people, the devil—are not godly fears. They are counterproductive. That is why the words *fear not* and *do not be afraid* are spoken over and over again in the Bible.

God told Abram, "Fear not, Abram: I am thy shield, and thy exceeding great reward" (Gen. 15:1, KJV).

He told Gideon, "Peace! Do not be afraid" (Judg. 6:23).

The angel Gabriel told Mary, the virgin, "Do not be afraid, Mary, you have found favor with God" (Luke 1:30).

God sought to quell these people's fears because He had a plan to fulfill in and through their lives. He knew that if their fears went unchecked, they might be talked right out of their destinies. Worse, they might have walked away from God's larger plan for His people.

Do you remember the No Fear T-shirt that first appeared in the late 1980s? It was designed for folks involved in action sports like motocross, surfing, and auto racing.[2] To participate in these sports, you need a healthy respect for the danger involved. If you take the risks too lightly or believe yourself to be immortal, you will overlook important information and make the kinds of mistakes that could cost you life or limb.

On the flip side of that coin, you cannot succeed in these sports (no less *enjoy* them) if you are terrified of everything that could happen.

That is an unhealthy form of fear. If you dwell on it, you begin to believe in the worst possible outcomes. In fact, it can affect your focus to such a degree that the odds of accident or injury increase.

There is a spiritual reason why unhealthy fears are so detrimental: they are the opposite of faith. Hebrews 11:6 says that "without faith it is impossible to please God, because anyone who comes to him must believe that he exists and that he rewards those who earnestly seek him."

A pure, godly fear of the Lord will keep destructive fears in check. When you reverence Him, you see things in a more positive light because you are convinced that God is both mighty and loving. He is able and faithful to walk with you through whatever fires might flare up in your life.

I say all this knowing that I have not *arrived* in this area. I have had moments of fear and worry. I have shared some of them with you already. There are others. When I was preparing to record my first solo album, I knew it would be a departure from my Crabb Family years. God had not sent us on individual paths for us to do things exactly as we had always done them. He was *stretching* us.

Speaking for myself, I knew there was more to this stretching than just taking on new responsibilities. There was going to be a stretching of my musical boundaries too. It was exciting to step outside the box, but it was also intimidating. I had so many questions. Some of them kept me up nights: Which songs are right for the album? Would my audience accept new sounds? Would this record be compared to those we made as the Crabb Family? Would the album measure up?

This was not motocross. I was not taking my physical life in my hands. But I was stepping out into new realms. There was the sense of being out on a limb and unsure whether it would hold my weight. A lot of what I had learned would continue to serve me well, but I also needed to access new information. There was a lot on my plate; it was more than I felt equipped to handle.

The truth is, I wasn't really dealing with my abilities and short-comings. They were not the issue. What I was dealing with was an attack of fear. And here's the thing about it: fear will challenge every forward step, and it will always arrive right on time. That doesn't mean we are doomed. If we remain alert to the enemy's tactics, we can bring truth back into focus and remember who brought us to the party in the first place. Nobody enters a new chapter of opportunity like the one I had entered unless God is behind it all.

The watch on my wrist reminded me of that. I did not need to prove myself or become perfect. All I really needed to do was to reverence the Father and follow Him wherever He would lead. And where He led me—oh, my Lord—it is more than I could think or ask!

FOLLOWING WHERE HE LEADS

When the time came to begin work on my solo album, God put the pieces together perfectly. First of all, my bandmates were an enormous encouragement and support. David and Lorie Sikes (our road manager and bass player, respectively) had been with us for years. When the winds of change blew in, they threw in their lot with me and have stuck with me through thick and thin. Justin Ellis, our keyboardist at the time, and Michael Rowsey, our drummer, were of the same mind and heart. Everyone in the band was excited about the solo album.

The team God formed on the recording side was outstanding, from our record company (Spring Hill Music) to everyone in the studio and beyond. I got to work with some of the best talent there is and enjoyed the most amazing relationships, both musically and personally.

With producers like Norro Wilson and Tommy Sims, anything is possible in the studio. Norro has produced for people like Charley Pride, George Jones, and Reba McEntire, to name a few. He has also written hit songs for folks like Charlie Rich and Tammy Wynette and worked with the likes of Shania Twain and Kenny Chesney. Norro is an artist; he knows what makes for a good vocal, and he understands the importance of choosing the right songs.

Tommy Sims is another amazing producer and a powerhouse of a bass player and songwriter. Tommy has worked with people like Bruce Springsteen and Michael W. Smith and written for artists such as Eric Clapton ("Change the World"). That is just the tip of the iceberg of Tommy's career. I loved to watch him in the studio. Just listening to him play his bass had an effect on my approach.

As the pieces fell into place, Norro introduced me to Neil Thrasher, yet another outstanding songwriter. Neil has written for Rascal Flatts, Montgomery Gentry, and others. Some of his songs were just such a *fit* for me. Singing them was easy in the sense that my own heart got wrapped around them.

I was also blessed to work with Tre' Corley. Tre' is so versatile; he would jump in wherever needed, whether to mix tracks or assist in the production effort. And Ben Fowler—we also had the benefit of his gifts in the studio. He mixed some of the songs the way only he can. I could go on and on. Vince Gill—yes, Vince Gill—sang on the album. Other greats contributed their talent, including Sonya Isaacs and the Gaither Vocal Band. I cannot begin to say how much it meant to work with all these folks. It was a wonderfully mind-blowing journey! No one could have had it better than I did making the solo record.

By God's grace, I took the journey one day at a time. My fears fell away, and God's plan came together every step of the way. The enemy tried to knock me off this glorious path, but God kept me on the straight and narrow with Him.

The album that caused me the greatest concern would prove to be a far greater blessing than any of us could have imagined!

Fear not, little flock; for it is your Father's good pleasure to give you the kingdom.
—LUKE 12:32, KJV

HOW TO SPEAK TO WALLS

When you come face-to-face with fear, it is like hitting a brick wall. If fear has a consistency, that is it. It is a wall just high enough, hard enough, thick enough, and long enough to jam your trajectory and block your entrance to your promised land. In fact, that is fear's job description: stop the kingdom and keep the people of God from entering into God's plan. It is a job description written by Satan himself.

How can I say that? It is simple. According to Scripture, "God is love" (1 John 4:8, 16). First John 4:18 goes on to say, "There is no fear in love. But perfect love drives out fear, because fear has to do with punishment. The one who fears is not made perfect in love."

God does not direct us to fear anything or anybody but Him. Instead, He draws us in love and moves us toward increased faith in Him. He will forever urge us to shatter the walls of fear and march into whatever promised land He has prepared for us. Walls don't intimidate God. He always sees what is beyond the wall and beckons us to join Him there.

That said, God never ignores the walls we face. He just directs us to get after them. He has a plan for every obstacle; He is an expert at tearing down impediments. Shortly after the Israelites crossed the Jordan, God told Joshua how to bring down the walls of Jericho and take the city:

> Then the LORD said to Joshua, "See, I have delivered Jericho into your hands, along with its king and its fighting men. March around the city once with all the armed men. Do this for six days. Have seven priests carry trumpets of rams' horns in front of the ark. On the seventh day, march around the city seven times, with the priests blowing the trumpets. When you hear them sound a long blast on the trumpets, have all the people give a loud shout; then the wall of the city will collapse and the people will go up, every man straight in."
>
> —JOSHUA 6:2–5

God instructed Joshua and the children of Israel in great detail. He gave them a seven-day plan: For six days, they were to march around the city once per day. On the seventh day, they were to march around the city seven times, blow their trumpets, and shout. (Try to imagine how peculiar God's directions looked to the average Israelite!)

We know what happened on the seventh day—a formidable wall fell flat to the ground, and Israel entered Jericho. What intrigues me most about the Jericho story is God's instruction about when the Israelites should shout. They would quietly circle Jericho twelve times, but on the thirteenth time, they would raise a ruckus.

Nothing God does or has recorded in Scripture is by accident. Therefore, I believe the timing of the shout is significant. Remember, Israel wandered in the wilderness for forty years as a result of their grumbling. They murmured and complained at every turn. They even asked to go back to slavery in Egypt! (See Exodus 14:12.) Except for Joshua and Caleb, none of the millions of Israelites who left Egypt made it into the Promised Land. (See Numbers 14:26–32.)

You have to wonder why God instructed the Israelites the way He did. I suspect it was because He knew their tendencies. God fully intended to give them the Promised Land but could not trust them 100 percent to set their nasty, old ways aside. Maybe God was saying, "I don't want them to blow this thing. I'll just tell them to keep their mouths shut."

God knew how intimidating that wall was. It was no slice of sheet rock; it was a solid structure yards thick. That is how the walls in our lives look. They seem so thick and so high that we feel at a loss to even believe they can come down. That is when fear takes opportunity. It grips the heart and says, "No way, no how. You might as well quit now and cut your losses."

Yet God says, "You are going through to the other side. Just keep walking, and say only what I tell you to say."

God sees walls differently than we do. To us, they are obstacles. To God, walls are the raw material for bridges. He shows us how to knock them over and use them as stepping-stones. What once kept us out becomes our pathway to the promise. We just need to believe God's Word, speak His Word, and praise Him.

By speaking faith instead of fear, you reconfigure the walls you face. When you are weary or worried, speak His Word or stay silent. Stay focused on Him, knowing that the walls will come down because He is the One who prepared your promised land in the first place.

LIVE LIKE YOU MEAN IT

This chapter started with a blunt statement: *Life is short.* It was not a defeatist statement. James 4:14 says, "You do not even know what will happen tomorrow. What is your life? You are a mist that appears for a little while and then vanishes."

No matter how long you live, this earthly life passes quickly. Every moment of it is precious, because we are precious in His sight. Merriam-Webster says that something *precious* is "of great value or high price."[3] You are a person of great value. Your purpose and dreams are of great value. What you were sent to this earth to do is of great value. Therefore, every cell of your being and every tear you cry matters to God.

And your price tag? It was *very* high. Jesus paid it with every fiber of His being, every thought in His mind, and every leaning of His heart. He paid it all, leaving nothing out. He prepared a place for you in this life and the next. He prepaid your ticket to peace, health, prosperity, and fulfillment. He gave you the desires of your heart and punched your ticket to their fulfillment. He gave it all for you, and He will see you through.

The enemy cannot compete with a love as complete as God's love. As long as you refuse to give in to him, he cannot override the Creator's plan, no matter how many dirty tricks, cunning deceptions, or full frontal attacks he attempts. In the end, it comes down to the choice that remains each day—either we will soak in our regrets and mourn over our failures, or we will live life to the full, regardless of the past.

Yesterday's wreckage is where it belongs—behind us. Today's walls are waiting to become bridges to tomorrow. Fear? It is nothing more than a fig leaf the enemy uses to conceal the greatness that lies ahead.

It is yours. Go ahead. Take it.

CHAPTER 8

GOD'S SHIELD OF PROTECTION

Just hold on, our Lord
will show up

And He will take you
through the fire again!

A LIVING REFUGE

IF YOU HAVE children, you know how hard you work to protect them and how much you are willing to do and give to keep them safe from everything and anything that might cause them harm.

Parental love is extreme. God's fatherly love is even more radical. Whether we realize it or not, He is always working to keep us safe and secure. His protection comes in countless forms. We tend to recognize the times when He has spared our lives from obvious trauma, such as an accident or illness or some other danger. We can see how close we came to disaster, and we cry out, "Thank God!"

We might not be as aware of the more subtle forms of His protection. How many times have the words of a friend or a spouse helped adjust your course? Can you think of a time when a minor change in plans—a missed flight or a *wrong* turn proved to be your saving grace? Even a broken friendship can be the means He uses to keep someone from a crooked path or outright destruction.

God's protection extends beyond what He does for us; it is about who He is. Read the words of the psalmist, and you will see what I mean: "He who dwells in the shelter of the Most High will rest in the shadow of the Almighty. I will say of the LORD, '*He is my refuge and my fortress,* my God, in whom I trust'" (Ps. 91:1–2, emphasis added).

The Lord does not just offer us refuge. He *is* our refuge. He *is* our fortress. We are invited to dwell in God—to climb under His shadow, to live in Christ, and to find the ultimate shelter in the Almighty.

Delight in God, Who Delights in You

Do you remember when we read Job's story of suffering, faith, and deliverance? He endured unspeakable trials, yet he came out of them more blessed than he had ever been.

Job knew how to dwell in the "shelter of the Most High." Job had never seen God or heaven or the angels, yet he knew God's voice. Job did the one thing God asks of us above all others: he worshiped his Creator. Job 1:1 says that Job "feared God and shunned evil." He was a man of integrity. He prayed and offered sacrifices to sanctify his family. He cared about the well-being of his children, even when they seemed to be less aware of God than he would have liked. (See Job 1:5.)

Job knew who his provider was.

When Satan questioned Job's motives, God allowed him to test Job. In the end, Job prevailed. Unlike Satan, Job had obeyed God's commands. Satan had been created to worship God, but Job actually did it. Therefore God protected him. It was almost as though God rubbed Satan's nose in his own mess, saying, "I chose you to worship Me from heaven itself. Instead, you chose to rebel against Me. Job has not had the benefit of seeing Me face-to-face, yet He loves and serves Me. Therefore you cannot defeat him."

As devious and cunning an enemy as he is, we are the ones who hold the key when it comes to Satan's schemes. Whether he will get what he came for is not his call to make. It is ours. Job went through a period of confusion over the trials that befell him. The situation did not add up in his mind. Yet even in his uncertainty, Job maintained the upper hand. He might not have felt that way, but Job's actions and attitude toward God were the keys to his deliverance.

Job's faithfulness reminds me of another passage from the Ninety-First Psalm:

> "Because he loves me," says the LORD, "I will rescue him; I will protect him, for he acknowledges my name. He will call upon me, and I will answer him; I will be with him in trouble, I will deliver him and honor him. With long life will I satisfy him and show him my salvation."
>
> —PSALM 91:14–16

That is so encouraging to me! God hears our prayers; He hears our cries. He heard the heart of Job, and He loved Job. God said Job was a blameless, upright man. (See Job 1:8.) God loves us too. He is blessed when we worship Him. He regards our love of family and of all people. He cares intimately about our salvation. He honors a godly lifestyle. There is nothing about us that escapes God's awareness and love. Jesus said, "Even the very hairs of your head are all numbered" (Matt. 10:30).

God delights in His people who have never seen Him face-to-face but believe and trust Him and praise Him by faith. God's love and attention are focused on us!

ANGELS ON GUARD

My family and I have had some unforgettable experiences on the road, including some encounters with extreme danger. One night while on the road in West Virginia, I felt something hit the bus.

Carl, our driver, cried out, "Oh, no!"

At first I didn't know exactly what had happened, so I went up to the front, near Carl. When I looked outside, I saw what he already knew: a couple driving in a small car had rammed into the front end of the bus on the side. As we began to get out of the bus, Carl warned, "Be careful. Those folks are acting like they are out of it. They may be on something."

Carl had the situation pegged. The woman who had been driving the car was high. Her dilated eyes and strange behavior gave away her condition. As bad a situation as it was, it could have been much worse. She and her passenger could have been seriously hurt. The impact could have thrown our bus off course. The possibilities for a tragic outcome were endless.

We called the police, thankful no one had been injured. While we waited for the police to arrive, I saw the male passenger from the car reach for something. Unfortunately, it was a pistol. I know many people carry legitimate weapons for protection, but this situation made me nervous. This guy was in no condition to make good decisions with a firearm. There was no telling what he might do.

As he got out of the car, he tucked the gun into the back of his pants. Then, for some reason, he brought it around to the front and said, "Let's see what happened to your little truck." I thought, "Man, he is worse off than I thought. He doesn't even know what he collided with."

This guy had just made contact with a forty-five-foot bus, yet he went on about our *little truck*. There was no way I wanted him to board the bus. I didn't know what was going through his mind, and I wasn't about to expose everyone on the bus to danger. We had babies and children with us. Some of them were still in bed; they didn't even know what was going on, so I tried to stay between him and them.

With the guardrail behind me and just two feet of available walkway between me and the embankment, I stayed with the guy. He started rambling; he was making no sense. Then he pulled something out of his pocket and threw it in the bushes. I assumed it was drugs, since he knew the police were coming. By this time, I was a nervous wreck. He walked around the bus and back to the car. Just then, we saw the swirling lights of the police car in the distance. I was still standing in that narrow walkway when he pulled out the gun and pointed it straight at me. I don't know whether he realized what he was doing. He was panicky and said, "Man, I've got to get rid of this."

A truckload of thoughts ran through my mind. There was no telling what would happen next. The police could not arrive and get out of their cars fast enough for my taste. Then, in an instant, the situation began to defuse. I said, "Man, it's gonna be all right."

We walked to the back of the bus, and he put the gun back in his waistband. The police had arrived by this time and already knew the man was armed. With gun drawn, one officer told him, "I understand you have a firearm with you. Put your hands up." The guy put his hands in the air, and the officer quickly restrained him.

That was one of the scariest incidents on the road that I can remember. I thanked God for the protection of His angels that night. When drugs are involved, people are not in their right minds. They can do things they would never dream of doing when sober. The situation was a mess, but God kept us through it all. He protected every hair on our heads.

For he will command his angels concerning you to guard you in all your ways; they will lift you up in their hands, so that you will not strike your foot against a stone.

— Psalm 91:11–12

God's Hand of Protection

If you spend enough time on the road, you are liable to witness crazy things. One night as we were driving down the highway, we spotted a car losing control on the opposite side of the road. It was traveling at a high rate of speed as it crossed the median and headed straight for our bus. Somehow the car hit the ground, flipped end over end ten or eleven times, and came to a stop without hitting us.

Everyone on the bus was fine, but it looked bad for whoever was in that car. We pulled over and ran to see whether anyone needed help. I honestly doubted that we could have helped anyone. I had a bad feeling in my gut and feared that we were about to find people dead in that car.

When we got there, we saw a guy with a flashlight. We asked him, "Is everybody OK in there? How can we help?" As I turned around, I saw another guy with a small cut on his head. He asked to use the flashlight. Then he crawled into the vehicle and pulled some drugs out of the glove compartment. He also grabbed a beer, opened it, and drank it right there while we waited for the police.

It turns out that he was the driver of the car that had jumped the median and flipped over all those times! He seemed virtually unharmed and completely oblivious to the fact that he had escaped what looked to be certain death. Unflustered, he leaned against the car and continued drinking his beer.

He might not have known it, but I was sure God was involved in the outcome. If that guy had hit the bus at the speed he was traveling, it would have been like hitting a brick wall. It could have been really bad for him and for us—but for God's protection!

You are my hiding place; you will protect me from
trouble and surround me with songs of deliverance.
—PSALM 32:7

ANOTHER KIND OF PROTECTION

God's mercy is so great that He desires to protect us even when we insist on going our own way. My grandfather on my dad's side lived a rocky life for a lot of years. He was good man, but alcohol had gotten the better of him. We loved Papaw, but we knew that only God could level out the rough patches in his path.

God did exactly that. It is clear to me now that God had His eye on Papaw on all along and had a plan—an awesome plan—to bring him into the sheepfold. Just about ten years before Papaw passed away, Dad had a preaching engagement scheduled during a revival. Papaw said he wanted to go to the meeting Dad was preaching and asked to ride there with us. He came along and brought an old tape recorder with him. Papaw taped the whole service, including Dad's sermon.

Only God could have written this script, because Papaw got saved at Dad's preaching engagement! You can just imagine how that blessed Dad and all of us. I know it blessed Papaw, because he went to every single night of the revival after that. He was a changed man, from the inside out. Papaw poured out his whiskey and never drank another drop.

Not only that, but he become the most soft-hearted man imaginable. You could walk into his house and say, "Hey, Papaw," and before you could get another word out, he'd cry just because he was so happy to see you. His last ten years were full of joy. His eyes filled up all the time. He couldn't hug you enough or get more excited about seeing his loved ones. It was an awesome thing to witness.

Papaw was a wonderful man. He worked hard with his hands his whole life long. He loved to fish too. He loved life more and more the older he got. Then he got sick. He didn't think much of it; Papaw figured he just needed a dose of penicillin to set him right. His doctor knew it was much more serious than that.

"Mr. Crabb," he said, "I've got some news. I'm sorry to say, it's not good news. Without a miracle, it looks like you don't have long to live."

Papaw had a bad case of lung cancer, yet he was so settled and content in God that he answered in complete serenity, "Doc, if it's my time, I'm ready to go."

Not long after that, Papaw stood up for prayer at church. Seven or eight months later, my siblings were on the school bus headed home. The bus went by Papaw's house. They saw an ambulance in the driveway and knew something was up. They were right; Papaw had suffered an aneurysm. The whole family ran to his side, but he was ready to go home. He had been for some time.

It was a sad day for us, but for Papaw it was a glorious trip home. The Father had snatched him out of destruction. God protected my grandfather when he was under the influence of alcohol and unable to protect himself. In the end, Papaw went home to heaven as a man whose heart was whole. He was a dear soul who loved people and loved God with all his heart.

It is so good to know that we will see Papaw in heaven someday. It will be wonderful to see his eyes glisten with joy at the sight of us. But Papaw's passing reminded me of something I needed to understand better: it is easy to take one another for granted. We can get so busy that we tell ourselves, "Tomorrow I'll visit Grandpa," or "Next week I'll give my loved one a call."

Often we assume that the ones we hold dearest, the ones who have invested the most in us, will be here forever. When they are gone, it is painful to say, "I wish I would have spent more time with my loved one. I wish I would have told this precious soul over and over again how much I really care."

A Birthday Wish

Now you know about both my grandfathers: Granddad, on my mother's side, and Papaw, on my dad's side. The Crabb kids have been blessed with the best grandparents. We couldn't ask for more!

There was a particularly poignant moment near the end of Granddad's battle with throat cancer. He was housebound at this point, sitting in a chair out front of the Smurf blue house he had built with his own hands. He said, "Jace, come here."

I did exactly as he asked, and he continued speaking to me.

"You know my time's almost up," he said. "I've done my best to instill in you the things a young man needs to know. Now it's time for you to do the same for your children."

Granddad had such a way with people. I listened intently, knowing we were sharing an important moment together and knowing that I would forever remember the things he wanted to say to me.

Granddad continued, "Jace, at first I didn't understand what you were doing traveling all the time. Then one day I saw you ministering on TV. I want you to know how proud I am of you. I'm so proud that you are my grandson."

My granddad's words lodged in my heart. They meant so much to me, because he meant so much to me. It was a perfect moment outside that blue house where Grandma had prayed for so many neighbors over the years and where I attended some of the best church services in my memory. It was another of God's precious stamps of approval. Granddad's words told me one more time that I was on the right track. I knew that God was involved in every step, even when my steps did not seem to make logical sense.

After a concert on the night of March 2, 2007, I prayed an unusual prayer for Granddad. It was the day before my thirtieth birthday. I climbed into my bunk on the bus, stared at the wall, and asked God to grant me a birthday wish.

Granddad was so sick by this time. I had visited with him the week before and knew he was very near the end of his life. He was confined to bed, suffering, and debilitated. I prayed, "God, please heal Granddad for good. He has fought a good fight and kept the faith all his life, so please let him go on home to be with You."

God showed me just how real He is and how closely He listens when we pray. About 10:30 the next morning, I received a call. "Jason, I hate to have to tell you this on your birthday, but Granddad has gone home."

I was sad about losing my grandfather, but I knew he had finished his course and was home in heaven. I gave God the praise knowing Granddad wouldn't have to suffer anymore. I remembered my prayer from the night before, and I knew God had answered it. I rejoiced knowing that Granddad got to see the Lord on my thirtieth birthday. It is a birthday present I'll never forget.

God's divine protection follows His children from the cradle all the way to the grave.

GOD'S AMAZING WAYS

Scripture declares God's amazing ways, saying, "Oh, the depth of the riches both of the wisdom and knowledge of God! How unsearchable are His judgments and His ways past finding out!" (Rom. 11:33, NKJV).

The longer I walk with Him, the more amazing His ways seem to be. There is no getting accustomed to His goodness. He just pours it out more and more with each passing day!

Just as this book neared completion, God poured out an enormous blessing, one I can barely wrap my mind around. Yet within just a couple of days of receiving this blessing, He began to reveal unexpected purposes in it. Bear with me as I try to explain it the way God has shown it to me. I will need to backtrack just a little so the story makes sense.

Over the years, the Crabb Family has been nominated for a number of Grammys. It is always a huge honor to be nominated. I can honestly say we were never disappointed when other people actually won the award. We just blessed them and continued on doing what God called us to do.

When my first solo album was released in 2009, it was well received, for which I am grateful. The drive has always been for our music to minister to people. The more popular the music is, the more it is heard. The more airplay and concert opportunities you get, the more hearts you can touch with the gospel!

What I never expected was to receive a Grammy nomination for the album. It doesn't matter how many times you have been there, a Grammy nomination is a big deal. In fact, it was overwhelming to me. With all the gifted artists out there and all the great music I hear, it is hard to imagine being given recognition by an industry of your peers.

Needless to say, Shellye and I, our family, and all those involved with the album or in our ministry were over the moon about the nomination. Before we knew it, we had to start planning a trip to Los Angeles, where the awards ceremony would be held. There was a lot of rejoicing going on!

I can't speak for anybody else, but I can say that I never expected to *win* the Grammy. It is not because I don't believe in the album. I do. It is the fruit of our God-given gifts and callings. We had surrendered all of it to His purposes. We knew the record was created in the mind of God to reach souls. Musically speaking and in every other way, I was happy with how the album turned out. It had been a God experience on every level.

Yet when they called my name at the awards ceremony, it was as though time stopped. A million things ran through my mind. I was so humbled and so honored, so stunned and off-guard. I remember thinking, "Lord, I know who I am. I am the least of all to be walking up on this stage."

In the midst of the emotions, I remembered when Donnie McClurkin had accepted his award years ago. I remembered the stand he took and how he testified to his faith in the Lord Jesus Christ. Now, on this day, Donnie and Karen Clark-Sheard had walked across the stage to accept a Grammy shortly before I did. There was something special about that!

At my manager Philip's urging, I had prepared some thoughts. He was right; you have to be prepared even if you don't expect to win. But when the time comes to accept the award, everything in your head seems to fall out. I paused for a moment to get my bearings and said a few words thanking my record company, my manager, my wife and kids. There were many more people I wanted to thank, but I thanked the Person to whom all glory is due—Jesus Christ—and went on my way.

He had given me another stamp of approval, another sign of the delight He has for His children. Winning was more than I could imagine, but not more than He could have ordained. His intent was clear: "Just keep on keeping on, Jason. You're going in the right direction. Keep following Me."

I don't know how long I shook after that. I do know that when I stepped behind the stage and walked toward the media pool, Donnie McClurkin was there waiting for me. What a class act he is! He gave me a big bear hug, and we took a photo together. It was a sweet moment. We talked a little bit and then went on to talk to the media folks who wait to interview the winners as they exit the stage.

It was an exquisite day—yet one that had a bittersweet tinge. I wished that the whole Crabb family had received that award. We worked so long and so hard together, and I learned so much ministering with them. I knew this Grammy was my family's as much as it was mine. It was hard to reconcile that in my mind, especially at first. Yet as conflicted as I was about whose name was on the award, everyone in the Crabb family rejoiced with and for me. I am truly a blessed man.

So what has the Grammy got to do with God's protection? You will see in a moment how winning an award set the stage for a bigger, more important miracle. God had something special in mind long before I was nominated.

GOD'S EXTRAVAGANT LOVE

Six of us traveled to Los Angeles for the Grammy Awards: Shellye and I; her sister Kellye; her husband, George; and Philip, my manager, and his wife, Tina. We stayed in L.A. a few extra days, enjoying a short break and some of the sights.

A day or two after the awards program, a young man walked up to me out of the blue and said, "I've seen you on TV."

I never know quite what to say when people recognize me from television appearances. Like most everything else that involves God's calling on my life, it is humbling. I stammered something, and he went on speaking.

"You're on that Christian channel. I used to watch you all the time when I was in prison. Your ministry blessed me over the years."

I was taken aback to think how much a few minutes of ministry can mean to someone you don't even know. I asked him how things were going for him. He looked down for a second and said, "I've had a hard time getting my feet under me now that I'm out. I'm getting some help, but—"

I looked the man in the eye and saw the potential God had wrapped into his being. I said, "You know that God has great things in store for you, right?"

"I just can't see that right now," he replied with remorse.

"Let me tell you something," I said. "God has *great things* in store for you."

We spent a few more minutes talking. I encouraged him all I could and realized something. By all appearances, we had come out to L.A. for the Grammy Awards. Now I believe that the real reason we were in Los Angeles was to give someone hope. God gave me the privilege of meeting a dear brother who just needed a sense of the bigger picture.

I thought, "Lord, if the Grammy was Your way of getting me out here, so be it!"

God's hand of protection is on that young man. God used Christian TV (how I thank Him for those channels!) to protect and nourish him with hope while he was incarcerated. Now God had arranged a new, unexpected way to impart hope to him as a free man.

God goes to great lengths to protect His children. He will bring two people together from opposite ends of the country, and even the planet, just to make sure one of them can say what the other needs to hear.

I believe God used me to encourage that young man. Whether he knows it or not, that young man encouraged me and reminded me of how perfectly God guides our footsteps.

He is so worthy of praise!

BUILDING A HEDGE

Lots of prayer has covered my family and me over the years. Prayers from long ago form a hedge of protection that continues to shelter us today. Grandma has played a big part in building that hedge. So have my parents, my siblings, friends, pastors, and even people I don't know. Prayer is powerful!

Prayer played an enormous role in Shellye and me being able to start a family. The obstacles were significant, but the day came when the miscarriages and sorrow were behind us. God made a way for our daughters to be born into this world, Ashleigh first and Emmaleigh a couple of years later.

Ashleigh and Emma (we call Emmaleigh *Emma* most of the time) are our two most beautiful miracles. Shellye and I love them so much! The children God gives you are always a blessing to be loved and cherished. Somehow, after losing two babies by miscarriage, we are even more strongly impressed as to just how precious our girls are.

Now that I am a dad, I pray a hedge of protection over Ashleigh and Emma, just as my parents and grandparents prayed one over me. There is nothing I would not do to keep them safe and well. Yet I know that even the best dad cannot be all that they need in life. Only God can care for my loved ones in the perfect and complete way they ought to be cared for. That's why I pray for them always and trust Him to lead me in my role as their earthly father.

That role gives me a lot of joy! It's a kick to be home with *my three women*. There is nothing better than coming off the road and walking into a house full of giggles and girl talk. Everything the three of them do blesses me up, down, and sideways.

I told you in the beginning pages that our daughters are as beautiful as their mom, and it is true. Like Shellye, they are beautiful in every way. They each have their own personalities and ways about them. It is such a treat to watch them grow and develop into the unique people God created them to be. They are sisters all right, but they are as individual as any two little girls could be.

Ashleigh just turned seven. Emma turns five later this year. Ashleigh is really good at being the big sister in our family. She was born with a mother's heart. She is as tenderhearted and gentle as can be. She loves to care for and pray for others. Her prayers bowl me over. She has so much insight—more than I can imagine having at her age. It is as though she can see right into the needs of others. She has so much love for people and for God that when she prays, I forget that she's a child. She prays like a mature adult.

Ashleigh isn't all about Ashleigh. Not that I would be surprised or upset if she were. There would be nothing unusual about a young child seeing herself as the center of her own universe. Part of a parent's job is to help children outgrow that perspective. But it is different with Ashleigh. She cares for everyone else and notices what others are going through. When someone is hurting, Ashleigh picks up on it. She is always ready to help.

Not long ago, the four of us went out to a favorite Nashville eatery. As we exited the restaurant, Ashleigh spotted a homeless man on the sidewalk. The contrast was stark: he looked worn down and lonely from years of hardship and isolation; we were refreshed by a good meal and family fellowship. I watched as Ashleigh took in the scene—and she took in every bit of it. As she watched the man and assessed his plight, he asked for money. I knew where her heart was, so I gave her a dollar. She put it in the man's hand.

It was an intense moment for her and for the rest of us watching her. As we turned to leave, Ashleigh continued to process what she had seen. She looked up at me with a million questions in her eyes. It didn't take long for the questions to come tumbling out: "Daddy, does that man have a family? Doesn't he have a home to go to? Is he hungry?"

I barely knew where to begin. I tried to explain that things can happen in a person's life so that they find themselves alone and living on the streets. We talked through several different scenarios. I don't think any of them resolved the issue for Ashleigh. She's the kind of kid who wants to understand how in the world something like that could be allowed to happen in the first place.

As she tried to make sense of it all, I told her, "Honey, that's why we tell you about Jesus. We love you so much, and we want to help you live a good life. We want to guide you away from the kind of difficulties that man is experiencing."

Ashleigh's wheels continued to turn. She listened to every word I said and asked, "So, Daddy, why didn't we tell that man about Jesus?"

I had no good answer to offer. I was so focused on what my daughter was going through that I didn't share Christ with the homeless man. To explain it that way would not have satisfied Ashleigh any more than it did me. Her big, tender heart saw nothing but the "Jesus bottom line": there was a need, and she wanted to meet it.

Right there, we stopped and prayed. Actually, Ashleigh prayed. She said, "Jesus, I am sorry I don't praise you more." Ashleigh is our little hedge-builder. To this day, she prays for the homeless and asks the Lord to provide them with jobs and whatever else they need to get off the streets and be as blessed as she is.

Both of my girls have a heart for prayer. Shellye called me in tears one night to tell me how the girls had laid their hands on a girl from their cheerleading squad. The girl was sick and was going to miss an important competition. The Crabb girls didn't want her to miss out on the fun. They wanted her to be healed!

ANOTHER BIG LITTLE GIVER

After Ashleigh was born, it was hard for Shellye and me to imagine loving another child the way we loved the first. (As the firstborn after two miscarriages, you can imagine how we spoiled Ashleigh.)

When we learned that Shellye was carrying Emma, we wondered whether we would have enough love to go around. We had yet to realize that we didn't have to work at making room for Emma. Instead, God was bringing Emma into our lives to fill the space He had already created for her in our hearts. When we saw her, we knew we had more than enough love for both our children.

The day after Emma was born, the doctors came to share the results of her newborn tests. All of her results were perfect except for one: her hearing test. The doctor said Emma's hearing tested at 30 percent of what they consider to be normal. The news was unsettling to me. It was even more upsetting to Shellye, who had just delivered and was dealing with all of the hormonal fluctuations women face after childbirth.

We did the only thing we could do right then: we prayed and left the issue in God's hands. That night, people came in and out of

Shellye's hospital room. At some point, someone let the door slam. Emma was in Shellye's arms at the time. As the door banged shut, the baby jumped. What a relief it was to see her react that way! We knew Emma's hearing was just fine.

Emma is four now, and believe me, she hears *everything*. One night before bedtime she wanted to make sure all the doors were locked at the house. I asked her, "What's wrong, Emma? Why do you want to check the doors all of a sudden?"

She replied, "I'm scared, Daddy."

I told her, "Baby, there's nothing to be afraid of."

"Yeah, there is, Daddy. There are burglars around. Aunt Leslie said so. What if she's right?"

I learned that Shellye and her sister Leslie had taken the kids to McDonald's that day. Leslie noticed that the Hamburglar was back in the store's advertising materials. She mentioned it to Shellye. Emma took it to mean there were actual burglars in town. Her ears don't miss a thing!

Emma has a strong, lively personality. She is very outgoing and open with her emotions. You never need to wonder what Emma is thinking; she is always ready to share her thoughts. She's a carefree little girl who also has a seriously giving nature.

Last Christmas we gathered with extended family for a gift exchange. All of the kids were excited about their presents and were busy playing with their new toys. One of the adults made what the children thought was a serious announcement: "OK, kids. We need to put our presents back in their boxes and give them to some other children."

For several moments, no one explained that this was just a joke. I watched Emma's reaction. Like any four-year-old, she was crazy about her presents. I knew she wanted to keep them. Yet she walked right up to me and said, "Daddy, who do I need to give my presents to?"

I was so touched by her willingness to surrender the things she loved so someone else could have them. It wasn't the first time she had responded that way in her young life. Recently Emma's class arranged a gift exchange. Each child was to bring a wrapped present to class and exchange gifts with another student. One of Emma's classmates had just had a death in the family. As a result, the child's parents had forgotten to prepare a wrapped gift. Emma was so torn up about it, she said, "Daddy, please get something so that boy won't be left out."

Emma is just as loving and protective at home. She loves her big sissy so much. And is she ever protective of her momma! Anytime Shellye and I have what the great gospel artist Jeff Easter would call "an intense moment of fellowship," Emma will get in the middle of it. Momma can say whatever she needs to say to Daddy, but if Daddy raises his voice the tiniest bit, Emma will say, "You don't need to talk to Momma like that, Daddy!" End of discussion. Daddy loses the argument. It goes with being the only male in the house (even Jazzy, our cat, is a girl). But I wouldn't have it any other way.

FOUR PEAS IN A POD

Each of our girls is definitely one of a kind. Still, they are sisters, and they have some things in common. Both of them have great voices and excellent pitch. Sometimes they come up on stage and sing with me using their little pink microphones. It tickles me to see them up there. They always hit the stage ready to go. Ashleigh is old enough now that she is more conscious of getting the song right; Emma on the other hand just lets it rip—right lyrics or wrong, she never holds back one bit.

Shellye and I feel like two of the most blessed people on the planet. God has brought us through many things and has shown us His goodness each and every day. He has protected us and even protected our dreams of raising a family. If all we had was the four of us, it would be more than enough.

Daily our daughters remind us of God's love. They are beautiful pictures of the lengths to which He will go to bless and keep His people. No matter what is going on, His strong hand continues to reach for us. He never abandons or disappoints us, and I know He never will. Whatever it is that God has in store for us, that is what we want. We know nothing else could compare.

We are content to rest in the shadow of the Almighty.

TRUSTING GOD

*I know within myself that
I would surely perish*

*But if I trust the hand
of God, He'll shield the
flames again, again.*

IT IS JUST as my dad wrote in "Through the Fire": within myself I would surely perish, except for the trustworthy hand of God. He is the only One able to carry my family and me through the ups and downs of the amazing life we are so honored and privileged to enjoy.

Thinking back to my childhood, I cannot remember a single blip on the radar screen that revealed the wonderful encounters awaiting me. I could never have foreseen the amazing people and divine moments God had lined up in my future. He is that good! God can take what looks like nothing and bring forth new life, even from a handful of dust. (See Genesis 2:7.)

He has been the *main character* in these pages, but He gave you and me leading roles. We are the "apple of his eye" (Deut. 32:10; Zech. 2:8), the ones from whom He withholds no good thing—*not one* (Ps. 84:11). He desires to lead us into blessing (Gen. 12:2). He is that kind of Daddy. It doesn't mean we won't go through things, but I can tell you this: even when life looks dark, there is light enough to take us through.

Your story is far from done. Your dreams can come true when you least expect them to. There are bright days ahead when your joy will be so full that it will poke holes through the ceiling, and you will dance like Grandma does! And on the days when you cannot walk another step, the Good Shepherd will be there to carry you over the rough terrain.

Charles Spurgeon said it this way:

> There is a blessed proportion. The Ruler of Providence bears a pair of scales—in this side He puts His people's trials, and in that He puts their consolations. When the scale of trial is nearly empty, you will always find the scale of consolation in nearly

the same condition; and when the scale of trials is full, you will find the scale of consolation just as heavy. When the black clouds gather most, the light is the more brightly revealed to us. When the night lowers and the tempest is coming on, the Heavenly Captain is always closest to His crew. It is a blessed thing, that when we are most cast down, then it is that we are most lifted up by the consolations of the Spirit. One reason is because trials make more room for consolation.[1]

His sense of balance is perfect, and His consolation is sweet enough to keep us. That is why I shared my hard times with you. Rough days are part of every life. They show how trustworthy He really is. They prove how far His love reaches. Like nothing else can, the fire reveals the depths of His goodness, mercy, and glory.

There is another reason for sharing the testimonies of difficult days. The devil tries to beat each one of us down with the idea that we are the only ones with a mess on our hands. That is a lie, plain and simple. You have been there. I have been there. Granddaddy and Auntie So-and-so and Moses and Paul have been through hard times too. That is what makes a testimony so powerful: we are reminded that there is nothing strange about tribulation and nothing impossible about the victory that follows!

His goodness is without measure. The Father never runs out of ways to bless His kids. The types of blessings vary from life to life and season to season. His stamps of approval speak to each of us in personal and intimate ways. In this season of my life, He is heaping favor in the form of industry awards. In the weeks since I was honored with my first Grammy, I have also been blessed with six new Dove Award nominations. I cannot wrap my mind around that. There are no words to explain what it *really* means to me. The important thing is that it speaks of Him, His goodness, and His plan in ways that I can understand.

He is never done pouring out His love. He is generous beyond anything I can imagine. He has only good things on His mind where we are concerned. He is a faithful Daddy, always ready to put an arm around your shoulder to say, "Son, daughter, you're the apple of My eye. You're right where I want you to be. Keep on walking. I'm right here beside you—and I always will be."

Sweet Surrender

One night while I stood on stage, I thought about the amazing path both behind and ahead of me. I realized the awesomeness of God's plan and the way in which He brought five ministries out of one! For fifteen years the Crabb Family Singers ministered around the country. We shared a single schedule and all the ministry opportunities our schedule represented. It was wonderful—intensely, indescribably *wonderful*.

Yet our God is not one to quit when the going gets good. On the night that Pastor Rod Parsley prophesied a time change and gave me his watch to symbolize the words he spoke, God made it clear that He had much more in mind. Today, Gerald Crabb Ministries, Crabb Revival, Aaron and Amanda Crabb, the Bowling Family, and I have five separate schedules. On any given night, you could find one or all of us ministering in different cities. We might be singing, preaching, or just shaking hands and sharing a word of encouragement with someone God has sent across our paths. The point is that He is a God of increase: He has multiplied the Crabb family's potential to reach souls *fivefold*.

In the end, it all comes down to what Grandma saw as she raised her hands to heaven on the day Granddad died. She kissed the love of her life good-bye and rejoiced in the outcome of his life's journey. That is the bottom line in everything we do. Through music, the preached Word of God, and any other door the Lord opens, we are called to share the hope of eternity with people everywhere.

When challenges arise, when things go wrong, when I miss my wife, my kids, my own bed, I remind myself of that hope and all that it means to precious souls. Whether we see six hundred souls saved at a festival (as happened in New Mexico recently) or have the privilege of encouraging a single brother on the streets of Los Angeles, it is the reason my family and I do what we do. It is what God has in mind for us. It was the very thing Granddad was proud of—he saw the generations after him doing what he had done his whole life. He saw us reaching out to others.

Back in the dark season during my teens, I could not see this day coming. My vision was blurred by the brokenness, bitterness, and frustration within me. But God saw this day! He reached down into my heart and stirred the ashes. He showed me His love, and suddenly, I remembered that He was all I needed. The full picture was not yet clear, but I caught a glimpse of a better life. It began with a simple prayer: "Here I am, Lord. I surrender all."

The ground of my life shifted that day. I learned that I was on this earth not to be influenced but to *be* an influence. I would come to understand that I was—*that we all are*—called by Him. My part was to share His name using the tools He put in my hand.

Once I rejected the rebellion that had driven me off God's path, He mended my brokenness, stitch by loving stitch. He did the same for my loved ones. We are firsthand witnesses to His mercy. There is no question: we have to share it!

Since that time, the Father has been teaching me how to let go and leave life's junk at the altar. He has given me a passion for those who want to do the same. He put a cry in my heart for the church to be free from the tyranny of bitterness, rejection, and betrayal. He gave me, my parents, my siblings, and our spouses a way to share His healing ways with others. He has allowed us to use our voices, instruments, and any other gifts we have to make His name and His love known. I can't think of anything I would rather be a part of than His work in the earth.

There's something else I'm sure of: there will be more seasons of change ahead. Change is part of taking up your cross and following Him. However many seasons are ahead, they are all chapters in the same journey. Even the changes we least expect are part of God's plan to lead us where He wants us to be. However uncomfortable life's surprises might be, they are signals of God's promotion. With each shift, He draws us up higher to a place where He knows we will need to trust Him even more.

It is a place of sweet surrender.

A Song of Thanksgiving

Early on I said this book was my song of encouragement to you. My tune has not changed. Let me *sing* it to you one more time with all of my heart: "Don't quit! The biggest and brightest blessings are on the other side of the struggle."

This book is also my song of thanksgiving. I give thanks for everything God has done for me and my family. The Bible says it better than I can: "Every good and perfect gift is from above, coming down from the Father of the heavenly lights, who does not change like shifting shadows" (James 1:17).

Jesus Christ wrapped every good and perfect gift two thousand years ago. Not a single aspect of redemption was left undone. Jesus did it all. He left us His Word and even earthly signs to help us understand all He did. Not too long ago, I went to the Holy Land with a dear pastor friend. We went to the sepulcher believed to be the place where Jesus was buried. The Scriptures came alive before our eyes.

As we stood before the tomb, we had to stoop to see inside. I thought of the verse that described the disciple I believe to be John arriving at the tomb and bending over to look inside. (See John 20:4.) I thought, "Wow! God not only loved us enough to send Jesus to die for us; He also highlighted every detail that would bring us comfort and revelation over the centuries. He caused John to mention the seemingly insignificant fact that you have to crouch to see inside Jesus's tomb!"

Everyone in our group was deeply moved as we stood outside the sepulcher. Before entering it, we took Communion together. Dear Lord, what a moment it was! When we stepped inside, my brother began to sing:

Crucified laid behind the stone
You lived to die rejected and alone.
Like a rose, trampled on the ground
You took the fall and thought of me
Above all.[2]

We stood holding hands and crying inside those walls, oblivious for the moment that people were waiting their turn to come in. I would have given almost anything to have spent more time there and to have the whole family with us.

The tomb underscored the finished work of the cross! Jesus did it all so that we could live it all, to the full. It is just as the angel said: "He is not here [in the tomb]; he has risen, just as he said. Come and see the place where he lay" (Matt. 28:6).

I am forever grateful that He thought enough of you and me to do all that He did for us.

From Here, Where?

The experience in the sepulcher branded my heart, yet I know that I am not called to live in the tomb. I have to step outside and walk in the direction of the future, confident that what Jesus did is more than enough to take me everywhere He has called me to go.

After receiving my first Grammy award, different people interviewed me. Someone asked whether the award had answered any questions for me or raised any new ones. I chuckled and said, "It definitely raises new questions. Once God blesses something He created, like He did this album, you can't help but wonder, 'Lord, where do we go from here?'"

Without the Lord in my life, that question would weigh me down. There is the sense of greater responsibility, the understanding that the bar has been raised and the status quo is history. Yet because of Him, the challenge delights me. We are human; we always wonder what is next. But with a Father like Him, we don't have to worry or wonder. We can simply trust that God is directing and blessing our steps!

From here, where? I don't really know. But I'm not worried about it either. If I get nervous about things in the days ahead, all I have to do is look back to the fidgety times in my past and know that every one of them led somewhere good. Every card that was dealt me and my family served a purpose, even if we didn't think so at first. So whatever the future holds, I can leave it in His hands and say, "Here I am, Lord. Where are we going today?"

THE SONG CONTINUES

How can I thank Him enough? There are no words to describe the sense of wonder that stirs in my heart every time I think about the truth that the living God has His hand on your life and mine. Maybe the best way to thank Him is to count my blessings and express my appreciation to the people who are in my life because of Him.

At the top of my list is my bride, the love of my life, and the mother of our children. Honey, you have made me the man I am today. You motivate me and the girls to press on. You bring out the best in the three of us. I don't tell you often enough how crazy I am about you. You are the one I can pour out my heart and soul to without fear or shame. I appreciate that *so* much more than I can explain with words.

Heaven knows you took on a tall order when you married me. Few women would be willing to pay the price you pay every day for the calling that is on us as man and wife. I can't imagine anyone else doing it with the grace you do. You are the perfect mother to our girls. You are the woman of my dreams.

Ashleigh and Emmaleigh, it will take your mother and me the rest of our days to tell you how much joy you have brought into our lives. I thank God for every little thing about you and for the love that you show to others. My prayer is for you to fulfill your callings in life as you come to know Christ more and more each day. God has created you to make a difference in this world, to help others, and to encourage those who are in need. Already you are demonstrating the love of Christ everywhere you go. I am so very proud of you!

To all of the Crabb clan—where can I begin? Your love has molded me over all these years. Being around you and working with you has helped me to become a man who desires to fulfill his calling in life. To my parents and grandparents, thank you for the heritage you imparted to us kids. The foundation you laid has kept us all these years! To my brothers and sisters, you are my best friends in the world. We have experienced so many things together, so many more than one book could tell. I am a better person for watching your lives and being challenged by you. I am so grateful to call you my family. Among my highest hopes is for every one of your dreams to come true in Him.

To David and Lorie Sikes—David, nobody can keep us road warriors on point like you can. Your management and technical skills are out of this world. Lorie, you make your bass sing in every song, and all the behind-the-scenes work you do, well, "thank you" just doesn't cover it. You two formed a rock-solid core for this ministry. Working with you each day is like being with family. Your dedication and sacrifice all these years—and especially through times of transition and even sorrow—mean the world to me. By myself I could never have successfully crossed the line God drew in the sand; with you, I know the music and the mission will be fulfilled.

Michael Rowsey—thank you for keeping that steady beat and for helping the rest of us tow the musical line! And to Justin Ellis, thank you for being there for us year-in and year-out. We will miss your blazing keys and your road savvy. May your new assignment be fulfilled with all the grace and glory of God in the days ahead.

Philip and Tina, I thank God for bringing you into my life! It is hard to imagine a time when you were not part of my family. Your love, wisdom, and perseverance keep me tracking and trucking every day. No one but God could ever keep a proper record of all the things you handle for the rest of us. Your willingness to pour yourselves out for God and to us boggles my mind. It is only by His grace that I could have the two of you beside me in this walk. Your love, dedication, and hard work inspire me daily! I am grateful for your honesty; I rely on it and you so heavily. How can I thank you enough?

To everyone who has ever come to one of our concerts, purchased a CD or a T-shirt (or this book), shared a word of encouragement, or partnered with us in any way—you mean so much to me and to this ministry. You are part of everything we do. Not a single soul is won for Christ without your support. When we all get to heaven, we will share the same amazing reward, and we will sing together for all eternity! I am so grateful to know that you are standing with us. Your love and support have opened the door for everything I have been blessed to be and do in this life. You are always in my prayers!

NEW THINGS AHEAD

I love my Bible, but I'm no theologian. I'm a gospel-believing, gospel-singing, gospel-preaching Kentucky boy who knows this for sure: God hasn't changed His tune where you are concerned. Not a day goes by that He isn't singing over you "songs of deliverance" (Ps. 32:7). Not a day passes without His ear being pressed to the ground of your heart. The Lord Jesus Christ is interceding for you even now (Heb. 7:25). He cares about your every breath.

God Himself created you. He has written the lyrics of your life with His own hand. They tell of an amazing future, a destiny paid for with the life of His only-begotten Son. Your potential has never diminished even one bit, no matter how your life story has played out so far. His song over you never changes, not even when the fire is raging and circumstances seem to contradict His perfect plan.

Wonderful things await you. They are designed to fulfill His dreams and yours. They may not come easily, but God's grace is enough to get you there. On any given day, He will pour out everything you need to walk the walk. When you lay your head on the pillow at night and when you open your eyes each morning, He will whisper to you about the new things He has planned. He will make "a way in the desert and streams in the wasteland" just for you (Isa. 43:19). He will do it all because He loves *you*.

The same God who has taken me by the hand has also taken your hand in His. He will see you through the fire, and He will take you places only He could prepare for you. Whether Jesus returns tomorrow or tarries, you and I will rejoice over your story in heaven someday.

It will be *amazing!*

NOTES

CHAPTER 1—FACING LIFE'S QUESTIONS

1. Neil V. Rosenberg and Charles K. Wolfe, *The Music of Bill Monroe* (Champaign, IL: University of Illinois Press, 2007), xii, found at Google Books, http://books.google.com/books?id=PmiFb1e1Fm4C&pg=PT383&dq=bill+ monroe+biography#v=onepage&q=father%20of%20bluegrass&f=false (accessed December 4, 2009).

CHAPTER 2—FACING WEAKNESS AND FRUSTRATION

1. *Merriam-Webster Online Dictionary*, s.v. "frustration," http://www .merriam-webster.com/dictionary/frustration (accessed January 20, 2010).
2. Enotes.com, "Bill Gaither: Singer, songwriter, producer," http://www .enotes.com/contemporary-musicians/gaither-bill-biography (accessed February 25, 2010).
3. "Sometimes I Cry," Gerald Crabb, © Copyright 2009. Gerald Crabb's Songs/BMI/Christian Taylor Music/BMI, a div. of Daywind Music (admin. by EverGreen Copyrights). All rights reserved. Used by permission.

CHAPTER 3—FEELING ALL ALONE

1. Herbert Lockyer Sr., ed., *Nelson's Illustrated Bible Dictionary* (Nashville: Thomas Nelson, 1986), s.v. "seven."

CHAPTER 4—FINDING HIS STRENGTH IN MY WEAKNESS

1. "The Shepherd's Call," Gerald Crabb, © Copyright 2004. Christian Taylor Music/BMI, a div. of Daywind Music (admin. by EverGreen Copyrights)/ MPCA Lehsem Songs (admin. by MPCA Music, LLC)/BMI. All rights reserved. Used by permission.
2. Lawrence Chewning and Ray Boltz, "The Anchor Holds," Word Music/ ASCAP (a division of Word, Inc.) and Shepherd Boy Music/ASCAP, 1999. Print license applied for.

3. Billy Graham Evangelistic Association, "Billy Graham Wakes Up the City That Never Sleeps," June 27, 2005, http://www.billygraham.org/mediaRelations_pressReleases.asp?pr=176&src=6 (accessed February 25, 2010).

4. Ibid.

Chapter 5—Counting the Cost of Christianity

1. Sue Monk Kidd, *When the Heart Waits* (New York: Harper Collins, 1992), 87.

2. Roland Bainton, *Here I Stand—a Life of Martin Luther* (Peabody, MA: Hendrickson Publishers, 2009), found at Google Books, http://books.google.com/books?id=IwyGxoDKk1wC&printsec=copyright&source=gbs_pub_info_s&cad=3#v=onepage&q=Next%20to%20the%20word%20of%20god&f=false (accessed September 3, 2010).

Chapter 6—Divine Help in Desperate Times

1. *Biblesoft's New Exhaustive Strong's Numbers and Concordance with Expanded Greek-Hebrew Dictionary*, CD-ROM, Biblesoft, Inc. and International Bible Translators, Inc., s.v. "*towla*" (OT 8438) and "*skolex*" (NT 4663).

2. Matthew Henry, *Matthew Henry's Commentary on the Whole Bible*, CD-ROM, PC Study Bible Formatted Electronic Database, Biblesoft, Inc., 2006.

Chapter 7—Refusing to Give In to the Enemy

1. *Biblesoft's New Exhaustive Strong's Numbers and Concordance with Expanded Greek-Hebrew Dictionary*, s.v. "*yir'ah*" (OT 3374).

2. Nofear.com, "About No Fear," http://www.nofear.com/page_usa.asp?itemid=102 (accessed February 25, 2010).

3. *Merriam-Webster Online Dictionary*, s.v. "precious," http://www.merriam-webster.com/dictionary/precious (accessed February 11, 2010).

Conclusion—Trusting God

1. Charles Spurgeon, *Morning and Evening*, CD-ROM, *PC Study Bible* Formatted Electronic Database, Biblesoft, Inc., 1999, 2003, 2006.

2. Lenny LeBlanc and Paul Baloche, "Above All," Integrity's Hosanna Music/Len Songs Publishing, 1999. Print license applied for.

For more information about the ministry
of Jason Crabb, please visit

www.JasonCrabb.com

or write

Jason Crabb Ministries
79 Elm Lane
Dyersburg, TN 38024

FREE NEWSLETTERS
TO HELP EMPOWER YOUR LIFE

Why subscribe today?

- ❏ **DELIVERED DIRECTLY TO YOU.** All you have to do is open your inbox and read.

- ❏ **EXCLUSIVE CONTENT.** We cover the news overlooked by the mainstream press.

- ❏ **STAY CURRENT.** Find the latest court rulings, revivals, and cultural trends.

- ❏ **UPDATE OTHERS.** Easy to forward to friends and family with the click of your mouse.

CHOOSE THE E-NEWSLETTER THAT INTERESTS YOU MOST:

- • Christian news
- • Daily devotionals
- • Spiritual empowerment
- • And much, much more

SIGN UP AT: **http://freenewsletters.charismamag.com**

8178